FARRAGO

A Memoir of Markie and ME

DIANA ROBERTS

ISBN
978-1-957378-94-7 (Paperback)
978-1-957378-93-0 (eBook)

God shall give the angels charge over you,
to keep you in all your ways.

Psalm 91, Book of Common Prayer

Preface

Farrago is a word that means a confused mixture. It comes from the Latin *farragin*, meaning mixed fodder or mixture, a word first used in language in 1632. Chiefly the Brits used it to express that something was a mess, a muddle, a knot, a snarl or a tangle on many levels.

This memoir of the relationship between my mother and me is just that, a *farrago*. Free of a positive or a negative judgment really, just a murky muddle. While I only lived with my mother for a short period of my life, the impact, a kind of aura from her, was always with me. I wanted to share this experience with anyone else who has ever lived in a family touched by mental illness. And I am sure you are out there.

For me, writing this book was like an exorcism. Something was hidden and dark way down inside me and the writing let it all out. I started writing during convalescence from a hip replacement in June of 2009 and finished this memoir two and a half years later. Now when I look at the manuscript on my desk I say to myself that's it, it is over and done and out of me. It feels great to have captured my mother's life in writing in a way that she can be remembered for a struggle that neither she nor I had any control over. If she were alive and ill today there would be many support systems to help her lead a normal life.

I hope this is a good read for you and for anyone whose family has been affected by mental illness.

Acknowledgments

To my husband, Bob Bray, who almost every weekend for two and a half years on Saturday morning would gently ask: "So, are you writing today?" Never pushing, only inquiring. To my great friend, Sidney Kenyon, who was the first person I dared show my erratic draft and who got back to me right away with a clear eye in the longest, kindest, most straight-shooting email critique that pushed me to move seriously to do the first revision. To my tennis companions Nancy and Dick Brickley who read an early draft. To Charlie Wyzanski, my high school classmate and longtime friend, who wasn't so sure about the future of a memoir like this, but urged me to keep at it just as he was wrestling with what and how to write about his famous father. To Daphne Abeel, a gentle editor who spent hours asking me just what did I mean by this or that comment. She was also a great help because we had the shared experience of attending the same independent girls' school in Boston. Thanks, too, to Anthony Sammarco, the noted historian of many Massachusetts towns, for taking a look at the manuscript. And most of all, I am grateful for the invaluable editing by Jim Kaplan, another high school classmate, whom I have only recently reconnected with after fifty years. This famous sportswriter, turned bridge and political columnist, spent way too much of his valuable time going through each line of my manuscript.

Many thanks to those kind friends who encouraged me while I wrote.

Table of Contents

A Short Hospital Stay

April, 2002

My mother, Markie, lay for hours on a stretcher in the hall outside the emergency room, waiting for a referral for treatment from the doctor who never came. It seemed so unfair to pass away on "diversion" from a bigger, better hospital. That is the term hospitals use for turning a patient away due to overcrowding in the ER. Perhaps it was because she had no insurance. It didn't matter. We got there too late after the doctor's call. By 2:30 a.m. she was gone. It was Marathon Day, Boston, April 16, 2002.

Markie was very sick anyway, but having to leave this world on a stretcher outside a treatment room seemed a sorry end to a long, mostly reclusive, sad life. She left behind three children whom she did not raise and who were as confused by her in death as they were by her in life. But even in illness, and mental illness, on her death bed and throughout her life, Markie Byron Roberts had style. In the end she went quietly, politely, and silently to the other side leaving us to wonder what her life, and our lives, might have been like if she had been with us all along.

My name is Diana. I was named for my mother's youngest sister, Diana Byron, whom my mother said was murdered at the age of 25. I am Diana Byron Roberts. I am the oldest of my deceased mother's three children, four if you count the miscarriage she had between me and my next younger brother, George.

My youngest brother, Cameron, stood next to our mother's lifeless head, weeping silently. My daughter, Page, was there, holding strong because she knew her mother did not know what or how to feel. George, our middle brother, was not there because he could never be in places where emotions might open up a floodgate of childhood memories. I briefly touched the hair and patted the face of the woman who brought me into this world. But I could not cry for the woman who never raised me.

There we were huddled together in a semi-private room next to someone who was comatose but not dead, at least not yet. Her face, barely visible above the stained white sheet and pale blue blanket, was the same color as Markie's bloodless blanched face. It was ironic that in death Markie looked the same now as she did in life. Her face, in life, always covered in white, white, white talcum powder, now in death seemed unchanged and inscrutable as that of a porcelain doll.

As if by design, the walls of the Needham Deaconess Hospital also matched the skin color of the two patients in the double room, except that the walls were peeling in many places, exposing plaster and iron pipes. Off and on I wondered about how my mother's face would peel underground and if the worms would render her pock marked and wrinkled like the decaying walls of the hospital.

The hospital in the early morning was completely quiet except for the sound of TVs left on by night nurses accompanied by the occasional beep of a bedside monitor. I felt as if I could hear IVs dripping everywhere, mocking the silence all around me.

A nurse's aide came by to close the curtains around Markie's bed to shield her roommate from what had just occurred. She told us we could stay as long as *we needed to*. I kept thinking that's what Markie did: she stayed as long as she needed to. Eighty-five years was a long time on earth for a woman who had been committed six times to mental institutions since her teens and had endured 36 shock treatments not by choice.

In her last days she talked about wanting to join our father George up in heaven. This was the last will and testament of a woman who claimed the biggest accomplishments in her life were divorcing her husband, not once, but twice and maintaining her strong stance against any belief in God. So what exactly did she really do with her time on this planet? She did not spend it much with me.

Several days before her death I sensed it was time to steal an afternoon from work to drive to Needham to visit her and to begin hospice care. I came with flowers and a smile, although inside I was very anxious about what was happening. The sun was shining through the curtain less window which was open, allowing in the fresh spring air. Tomorrow would be a great start for the Boston Marathon tomorrow if the weather held.

The nurse came by again, this time to say we could stay **as long as we wanted**. I could not wait to leave. I did not need to stay any longer. I left the room first and the others followed. The sun would soon be up

and the Boston Marathon would begin in Hopkinton. I wished I could be running the 26 mile race that day instead of having to face arrangements for my mother's farewell.

One Flew Out of
the Cuckoo's Nest

During the 1960s, when being institutionalized was often thought to be the optimum treatment for the mentally ill, Markie had moved rapidly in and out of residential mental institutions in New York. At twenty-two I was a college dropout busy escaping all responsibilities of an emerging adult. After a few odd jobs, I was lucky enough to join the Peace Corps in November of 1966. After three months of training in early childhood development at Wheelock College in Boston, I headed to New York and the flight to Tunis, the capital of Tunisia. Forty-four of us had made it through training and were headed for our "in-country orientation." We were going to set up day care centers in cities and towns all over Tunisia at sites built by a group of Peace Corps architects already in the country. We were called Tunisia Child Care 8. Later I would learn that we were the last Peace Corps group to train in the United States and not in the host country. It would be cheaper in the future to train volunteers in the country in which they would be stationed. There would also be fewer surprises from the very beginning of training and less attrition overall.

Just before the end of training my grandmother, Muffy, wrote from New York that she wanted to meet me in the airport in New York before my departure. At the time I knew that neither she nor I had any idea where Markie was although I thought she must be somewhere in New York City as she had no means to leave. I knew that Markie's only means of survival came in the form of a government disability check and that she must be picking it up regularly or at least have at a P.O. number. In her own way she was a survivor wherever she might be.

Muffy drove up to the airport parking lot in an honest-to-God pink Cadillac convertible that she had borrowed from a friend just for this visit. The top was down and even though I had not seen her since I was six when I last lived with my mother in the apartment above Muffy at 59 East 79th Street, I recognized her as my mother's mother. The salmon pink blouse

was the signature color I remembered of her as a child. She walked toward me where I sat in the section for those preparing for overseas flight.

"Hello, my darling, I am so happy to see you," she said. I have a gift for you to keep you healthy in that African country." She handed me a large heart shaped yellow box with Whitman's Sampler clearly marked in red script on the cover. *What a nice gift for my send off. Maybe Muffy wasn't so weird.* Muffy had surrounded the box with a red satin ribbon to hold the contents together inside. *Very thoughtful.* I pulled on the ribbon and lifted the box top.

"Wow," I stammered as I looked down on an array of several hundred multicolored pills. I am sure I seemed a bit stunned as I uttered my thanks. For a brief moment I contemplated the possible origin of my mother's early peculiarities.

"Vitamins, darling, vitamins! They are the key. You will need them, especially the Bs, to keep your body and mind whole and healthy," Muffy assured me as she picked out a red one and popped it in her mouth.

In another half hour, I thought, I would be gone and this woman would no longer be sitting next to me on this bench, too close for comfort. Then she started in: "I know you don't where your mother is or where she has been but I will tell you Markie has been in and out of a number of institutions in the last several years and up until recently had been living in a flea-bitten, rundown place called the Scott Hotel on the Westside. I have not seen or heard from her for months at a time in the last few years. One afternoon, about a month ago, in January, the phone rang."

"Hello, Muffy. It's Markie," my grandmother, who sounded much like my mother, reproduced the exact sound of Markie's voice as I remembered it. Old New York, aristocratic.

"You can't imagine the lump in my throat, Diana, to hear Markie's voice. All I can say is she didn't look as badly as I expected when I first saw her. She looked like she was eating better and had gained a little weight. Apparently she had gotten out of the horrible hotel and is now occupying that little apartment in Brooklyn that she once shared with your brothers. I have improved and furnished it. I am hoping at some point she can move into a bigger one, closer to me in Manhattan."

"Diana, I cannot pretend that she is well, but she is much better. I am sure most of the time she is fine. Some of the time she slips into what I call 'the bad moods'. There is a new book out on schizophrenia which describes the cause of the disease and its treatment. It asserts that it is a malfunction of the adrenal gland system—producing a poison in the patient's body which produces a chemical imbalance which in turn throws the brain and nervous system completely off base. The wonderful thing is that the two doctors who have done the research have found a vitamin that will restore the balance and repair the damage to keep the patient on an even keel. It will also prevent the disease from developing in persons who may be susceptible to the disease through heredity."

Here my attention began to fade. "It's very simple. Eat a high protein diet (practically no carbohydrates, no caffeine, no smoking and 3000 USP units (300 milligrams) of niacin (vitamin B3) daily. It is not expensive and is natural. I have not priced it as a synthetic, if in fact that exists."

Although Muffy had brought me all those vitamins to ward off any future demons that might come my way in Africa, clearly she was thinking about how to cure her daughter much closer to home.

"The problem now is to present it to your mother without connecting it to her trouble and prescribed for her by someone in whom she would have confidence. This has all come to me very recently and I am still waiting for the perfect opening. Meanwhile, I want you to know you need never again have fear the possibility of heredity because this defense is always available to you. I would be inclined to follow this diet pattern as closely as possible because, in any case, it's much the best diet for everyone. If you are interested I will send you the exact list of the high-protein foods in the process of my gathering all this information together."

Mentally I was beginning to scratch my head, wondering how long this monologue would go on when Muffy changed the subject.

"I want you to know, Diana, that your mother is thinking of you and brothers Teddy and Cameron all the time. She feels so much heartbreak because of the complete absence of communication for so long. When the birthday week comes along in the month of August when she and you and Teddy and Cameron all have birthdays, it is an agonizing eight days for her. That's about the time she starts trying to call first you, then Teddy and then Cameron. This week I managed to reach your stepmother, Joan, and asked her to tell Markie that you are 'abroad.' I knew this would soften the

blow for Markie when she could not reach you." Muffy seemed familiar with making up explanations.

"All girls seem to manage to go to Europe these days. However, she is now thinking you will return soon. When I spoke with your stepmother, Joan, she said Markie must be told where you are. I do not want her to ever know that I know where you are going and will not tell her. I know it would hurt her excruciatingly to know you left the country without seeing her."

"So please, dear, please sit down on that plane and write to her. That would be the kindest and greatest way for her to hear from you. Please say that you have heard from 'home' (not me) that she is living in an apartment in Brooklyn so you are sending the letter in my care. Tell her you did not let her know you were going to Africa because you felt it might distress her and that you have been so busy in training, etc. I know you will do this well."

"Whatever your contact has been with her since you were sixteen like that time for lunch in Boston at the Red Coach Grille with your brothers, she has completely forgotten. She thinks of you as you were as a baby and at three years old in the photographs of you I gave her to take to her apartment. The very first night in her apartment she put them next to her bed. I feel it is difficult for her to picture you all grown up. She still thinks of you as much younger. I suppose that is natural as that is how she remembers you." Another odd-sounding explanation.

"I'll be anxiously waiting for your letter to her. It's so important to bring her back into the real world from which she has been totally isolated for so long. She adores coming to my apartment near Central Park just to sit and remember the past when we were all together here, when you lived upstairs on the second floor."

We hugged briefly and said our goodbyes. At that point, I had no intention of writing. Muffy's last words were "I am so glad they are sending you to a city and not the jungle."

I moved quickly to put my bags in the line to get on the plane and to shut

Muffy's request out of my mind for the duration of the plane ride and for the foreseeable future.

Round Trip

After three months of training at Wheelock College in Boston to be a childcare specialist speaking Arabic and French, I was ready for my Peace Corps assignment to spend the next eighteen months in Tunisia. When I left Boston in February of 1967, winter was in full force. When I touched down in Tunis, it was warm and the palm trees were everywhere lining the streets. After a night of rest in a hotel where I would discover the next morning that my L.L. Bean penny loafers had been stolen, we took a bumpy, very speedy ride by bus to the Peace Corps home office in Carthage. I remembered from my fourth year Latin high school class that Carthage was founded by a woman, Dido, who fell in love with Aeneas. Dido's story ended in suicide caught up in the flames of a funeral pyre. That was Virgil's tragic tale of a lustful Queen of Tyre, in the epic poem the "Aeneid." Much less well-known is the legend, passed down in oral form, of a heroine who through courage and determination founded a city to rival Rome, and who refused to let herself be subject to men, even at the cost of her life.

The legend was not lost on me during our in-country training. Dido may have been a strong woman and a city builder, but I was definitely entering a patriarchal society where women were covered from head to toe with the burka and rarely left the courtyard of their homes. As a daycare worker I would have to become familiar with many family traditions that did not favor young women. In and around Tunis and Carthage and Sidi Bou Said, home, at one point, of the English spy Kim Philby, we visited a number of day care centers filled with the children of wealthy Tunisians and government officials. In the big cities my French proved efficient and effective. When I was told that I would be assigned to Sousse, the second largest city in Tunisia, about three hours from the capitol, I knew I would have to improve my command of spoken Tunisian Arabic.

My roommate, Terry, and I took up residence in Sousse in an old "marabout" we rented for the equivalent of $14 a month. The term refers to a Muslim hermit or saint and the tomb of the saint is called a "marabout." Our marabout had a bedroom with Dutch style beds built into the wall, half way up, one on opposite sides of the room. The beds were so large that they were almost like separate inner rooms within the bedroom. There was a living room, a kitchen with no refrigerator and a bathroom shower over a Turkish toilet that was barely more than a hole in the cement with a place to plant your feet and squat down. The rooms surrounded an open courtyard. Above the courtyard a narrow path ran around on top of the four square stucco walls of our house. The children next door often got on the top of their building and ran along the turret looking straight down into our courtyard at any time during the day. We were able to rent the place just as the architect assigned to build our jardin d'enfants was ready for us to begin registering children.

I met the mayor of the municipality at the yard just outside the jardin on my first day of work, as part of my introduction to my future charges that were between the ages of four and seven. Soon after I arrived at the site, I was greeted by a number of children coming off the street into the space to see what the new foreigner looked like. A little boy of about four and a taller girl of five or six approached me together.

"Huwa Hiya blank, blank, blankity blank" the girl said directly to me. I didn't catch the meaning of the verb in the sentence. I searched my brain to retrieve the right meaning from my three months of intensive training in Tunisian Arabic back in the States. I stared blankly at the girl, turned toward the boy and at last turned to the mayor who was chuckling by now.

"Excuse me, your Honor," I started in my best two-plus-Foreign Service-rating Tunisian Arabic, "I am so embarrassed. I am afraid I am inadequate and cannot translate what she said."

The mayor spoke decisively without even a trace of irony or a smile.

"The little girl just reported that the little boy told the little girl to *go fuck herself.*"

"Oh, sir, I did not learn that verb in training but I will look for it in the future," I said trying hard not to smile or to let on that I saw any humor in this incident. "I will see that Mounique takes a time out to consider the harsh language she has used."

Once the *jardin* was fully operating, I worked with two Tunisian assistants who helped me with the seventy children in the day care center, many of whom were not yet toilet trained. In Tunisia and other Arab countries toilet training is a matter of the child's readiness, not the parent's, to become fully disciplined in the habits of the toilet. And furthermore I was told the "Turkish toilet" is a much better invention than the Western "sit." In any case, I had my hands full most of the time keeping up with the children.

I acquired an ancient four door sedan and brought it into the yard just outside the classroom. I had my handyman, the "show-oosh", Mustapha, take the wheels off. Then we painted each of the four doors bright red, blue green and yellow. Some other men helped Mustapha plant the wheeless car in the sand, securing the doors open permanently so the children could go in and out of the car, bouncing off and on the seats and jumping into the sand, during recess and lunch break. I envied them and often wished I could join in their fun. But I was *the Directrice du Jardin D'Enfants,* not an *enfant.*

One day, the same child I had met earlier, Mounique, became quite ill with a stomach ache. I sent her home because I thought she might have appendicitis. When she subsequently died of a burst appendix, I visited the family to give my condolences. As I was leaving, the mother said to me, "Allah hi berik, God knows best. Besides, I have five other children. This one, the girl, will not be missed. One less mouth to feed, one less child to worry about." She spoke only in Arabic, not French, since she was poor and not educated. I was amazed and saddened by her lack of sorrow over her young loss, but it was just one of many lessons I was to learn.

I had little time to think about Markie, but when I did, Muffy's request that I write to Markie gnawed at my thoughts. I had received letters from her during Peace Corps training brought to me from home by Dad, but they were so jarring and so cloying in their salutations, that I don't believe I ever wrote back until I had been in Tunisia for a while. Finally I did begin to communicate with her.

In July I wrote to her bland news of my activities in July: things were going well; my language skills were increasing; and I was working with two Tunisian assistants who were teaching me many helpful things. I did not tell her about the child who died, because I could not imagine her

understanding the mother's reaction or the nature of life in the Third World. Then, just after Thanksgiving she wrote to me:

November 26, 1967

My little baby girl,

How absolutely, utterly divine to hear from you!

You know that to get your letter is the most wonderful thing on earth!

Now, darling, take it easy. Try not to put too much stress or strain into this. I know it's what you want to be doing. How courageous of you!

I am simply amazed and so proud of you my little angel!!!! I know you have a particularly great knowledge of children. And any children would be so lucky to be in association with you.

I worry about your going out with anyone while you are over there.

The best thing for you to do is not to go out at all. Go to bed as early as you

can and don't let anything interfere with your work.

One of the most difficult problems in international relations is the African,

as you know, and by keeping their children you are doing vital work.

I am continuing my studies of the insane. I am not doing any socializing.

I haven't in years as I'm plodding away at this thing that I'm interested in. I know more than anyone in the world on this subject.

I love you with all my heart my little baby.

You are the most precious little girl on earth and I am sure everybody knows.

With all my love
Your mother

Another letter came barely a week later.

December 1, 1967

"Diana, darling:

I gave a message for you over the phone to Teddy at the time of the birthdays. The best way to reach me (the way you sent your letter) is via my mother. To address the letter as you did is perfect. I have no phone here, trying to keep expenses down to a minimum. And also there is a   pack of criminally insane people here in the superintendent's office of the apartment that have fouled me up in a number of ways—including   stealing, and other things including taking my name off the mailbox. So, of course, I can never be sure of receiving a letter here. These people here   are a part of the whole apparatus of the criminally insane your father and   his secretary wife Joan are a part of—and some people all work together.

Well, my little baby, don't worry about these things. I am entrenched here and I'm saving a place for your little brothers, Teddy and Cammy, if they want to come down when you return.

Your very own Mummy

Even though I had not lived with her since I was nine, in a way Markie was always there with me. And letters like that did not help, because they were so bizarre, disturbed and disturbing. If I were back home, I would have, at some point, already had to deal with her, acknowledge her, be embarrassed by her, be scared of her, wonder if everyone knew about my mother. In Tunisia, I thought I was free. The children and my fellow Peace Corps colleagues knew nothing about Markie. Yet Markie was the virtual and constant Albatross in my presence. I often felt like Coleridge's ancient mariner who was plagued by the famous sea bird:

Ah! Well a-day what evil looks
Had I from old and young
Instead of the cross, the Albatross
About my neck was hung.

During that first year in the Peace Corps I felt myself growing up amid the mosques and imams, building a day care center under the hot sun of North Africa in the heart of Tunisia in the town called Sousse. With my two assistants and a doorman who said he smoked hash for his asthma, we were a hard working, happy gentle family. The group was supportive when I announced I would be on vacation for the next two weeks following the Christian Christmas holiday. They were glad that I would be seeing more of the rest of their country.

On December 26, 1967, early in the morning, I was standing in my office in my day care center, thousands of miles from Milton, Massachusetts. I was about to travel with my Peace Corps architect boyfriend, Alan, to Tunisia's more colorful neighbor, Morocco. We were somewhat anxious that, because Alan was Jewish, we would find travel difficult due to the then Israeli/Arab tensions.

The phone in my office rang: "Hello, HELLO! Operator, this is Diana's Aunt Martha, trying to reach my niece. Can you hear me? CAN YOU HEAR ME?!!"

Operator: "I am sorry. I have a bad connection. Can I get a message through for you?" "Diana, YOUR FATHER PASSED AWAY AT 9:15 YESTERDAY MORNING."

Yesterday? Christmas in the States. This could not be. We are going on vacation. There is no Christmas here. My father is not sick. He is an athlete. He writes me every week. I am his only daughter. He would not leave me. Not now. Not until this is over and I come home.

I put the phone down. I was at once numb and yet felt like vomiting, too immobile to cry or feel pain or anger. No phone calls or letters to let me know my father was ill with lung cancer in September and would die soon in three months. Now I knew why the last letter I had from him said he was paying the college loan for my one brief trial semester at Boston

University during the three years I was back in Boston after leaving college in the spring of my freshman year at Washington University in Saint Louis in 1963. He wanted me to find my way to return to college after Peace Corps debt-free, though my stepmother had always resented the expense. I suspended thought and got ready for the ride to Tunis and the 14 hour plane ride through Rome to Boston.

I left Alan and went home leaving my assistants in charge as they were already prepared for my absence. My roommate and colleague Terry, who had set up the day care center with me, had returned to the States back in the fall to marry one of the architects from an earlier group who had completed his two year service. I was glad to be alone that night.

The next morning I boarded the only *louage* I could find in Sousse at 5:00 a.m. and arrived in Tunis at the Peace Corps office three hours later. A kindly American office worker drove me to the airport. I didn't even notice the camel striding alongside the airstrip. I slept through the fourteen hour ride to Boston just in time for the funeral. Ted, my younger brother by three years, met me at the airport with half sister, Linda, whom I hardly knew because she was sixteen years younger and retarded.

"You know, our father died on Christmas," Linda greeted me in a high-pitched sing-song voice. Tears filled my eyes for the first time and ran down my cheeks as I forced myself to hold back any comment. Ted and others in the family always assumed Linda had no idea what she said or meant most of the time. They would say her condition excused her for acting like she was about to attend a fun social event that day. I didn't agree. I held indiscretions like this and others against her. I was often bothered by my feelings of resentment towards her because she was allowed to disrupt the family at inconvenient times. I believed she could be capable of discipline and better behavior if the family had better expectations for her. My stepmother always took Linda's side

After the service, the thirteen remaining days of my "Compassionate Leave" home from the Peace Corps in Africa were spent in a state of numbness, a blurring diet of three movies a day, making love as often as possible to a nice MBA candidate at the Harvard Business School, and sleep. At the end of the fortnight I was ready to get back on the plane to Sousse.

That's the kind of half girl, half woman I still was then. When I was four I learned to tie my shoes for safety's sake, in double knots, long before

others my age, to make sure I would survive loose laces, loose ends of any kind. One way or another I had been doing it ever since. Especially now. Neither death nor bad weather could make me give in to myself or anyone else when it came to staying on course.

My father taught me to be an athlete on the field and to think like one off the field. He was the one who played pitch and catch with me on the front lawn for hours at the end of the day after school. I could play offense or defense anywhere at any time. There was no doubt I quickly learned to be good at combat, with myself, as well as others. My father's death was not going to trip me up. I did not know at the time that I was just incapable of letting him go.

The louage screeched to a halt in front of my house that bordered on the main street of Sousse. I had arrived in Tunis at 5:00 am and boarded the first louage I could find that early in the morning. When I arrived in Sousse, shopkeepers were just opening up their stalls, the sun was not yet bearing down with intensity and my kindergartners were just beginning to hit the playground.

Today Sousse is the third largest city in Tunisia with a population of just over 160,000, about three hours south of Tunisia's capital city, Tunis. Located on the coast in the central east of the country, it borders the Gulf of Hammamet that is part of the Mediterranean Sea. Sousse has a long history, dating back nearly 3,000 years with a great deal of character. During my time there the government, under President Bourghiba, was beginning to develop the town as a tourist attraction because it had a great deal to offer, from its historic "Old Town" and "Medina" to the busy port and local sandy beaches. On many days in the late afternoon I loved to walk all the way across town to the beach to see ladies fully clothed bathing in the ocean with their long skirts spreading out in the waves around them in bright circles of color.

Sousse's medina was a place I visited almost every day since my marabout house was situated just above this section of the city. A medina is a wall-covered part of a city that contains many narrow and maze-like streets. The word "medin" simply means "city" or "town" in modern Arabic. Although it was not very large by Tunisian standards, the Sousse medina I knew was a charming and relaxed place, a pleasure for me to explore. The medina was full of tiny makeshift stalls where entrepreneurial Tunisians sold all manner of goods from bananas to burkas, the traditional dress of Islamic women. Bargaining for just about anything was an accepted, even encouraged, practice. Hustling was never a problem in the medina. Women could walk around safely and easily inside the walls, although we Peace Corps Volunteers were warned to look out for frequent "snab and grab" crime by petty thieves in the marketplace. A purse could be gone in a flash with the suspect nowhere in sight.

The main mosque in Sousse was built in 850 AD. Like its sister mosque in Karouan, it had, and still has, the outward appearance of a fortress. Unlike many other important mosques in Tunisia, the Great Mosque in Sousse has seen few major alterations over the centuries. The result is that, compared to other Tunisian mosques, it appears to be incomplete, especially as it has no typical tall minaret tower. In the 11th century, a domed building was added and this continues to serve as the minaret.

I loved the simple style of the mosque because it reflected the religious attitudes and lifestyle of the people of Sousse I knew then. The courtyard was paved with formal stone slabs separated by rows of broken paving set in the purple mortar. It sloped toward a central drain that collected rainwater in an underground cistern. There were wash basins for the ritualistic washing of hands before Muslims entered for worship. Surrounding the courtyard was a colonnade with arches supported by short square columns. A staircase in one corner led up to the ramparts, the domed minaret and an octagonal sundial.

The famous "Ribat" in Sousse was one of a series of fortified monasteries built along the North African coast in 821 AD as a fortress against the Christian marauders from Sicily. The word "ribat" comes from the same root as the North African name for holy men. Ribats of these times were generally connected to a very conservative and often ascetic practice of Islam.

The walls of the ribat in Sousse were made exceptionally thick because the town had no natural defenses. The ribat stands right on the Place Farhat Hached, apart from the many other crowded buildings in Sousse. It is surrounded by a broad paved area which allows visitors unimpeded views of the building.

That day, returning to Sousse, I definitely was not thinking about the town's historical significance or my good fortune to be stationed in such a famed part of North Africa. The flight back from Boston through Rome had seemed much shorter than the actual fourteen-hour trip home. On the other hand, the ride from Tunis in the louage felt like a lifetime compressed into three hours. I was sure my life expectancy rate went down every time I got into one of those breakneck speed taxis. It had been my experience that the Tunisian cabbies operated pretty much on auto pilot at 85 miles per hour from start to finish.

I was a wreck by the time I stepped out of the louage onto the street in front of the big knockers marking my double front door. Each knocker had some kind of animal design that worked out to be something you could bang on. Even though the doors were in front of me, I didn't really see them. But people passing by did, and frequently banged on them all day long whether I was home or not just to tantalize the American and keep her on her toes. I paid the taxi fee and decided I could not enter the house, be by myself, until the end of the day.

By now the children would be at the daycare center, the ***jardin d'enfants***, within the hour, all seventy-four of them in the two little windowless classrooms. The rooms were painted with cheery animals and pastel numbers, designed and donated by my artist friend visiting from the Netherlands. No matter how tired I was, I suddenly wanted to be there to let them know that I had not disappeared from their world, that Boston really was a place you could come back from in one piece. In my case, more like broken pieces. I wanted to let myself know I was not disappearing off the face of the earth. Why couldn't I feel? Anything.

As I walked past the tobacco stand and the pharmacy toward the daycare center, neighbors smiled shyly to welcome the Peace Corps lady back. One woman asked me: "How was President Johnson?" Another wanted to know if I had seen "Mrs. J.F.K. John Kennedy." Peace Corps volunteers were always VIPs to everyone but themselves, unless, of course, they got off on the all-Americans-are movie-stars kick. At this moment I wanted to be recognized by no one, except for the children. They had a right to have me back. Being with them would make me whole again over time.

"Shnihow-way-lik, lie-ilti? Laebes? How are you, children? Are you well?"

I prattled on as best I could for most of the day. If I could feel anything, I could feel that I had missed them. Mohamed's nose still ran like a faucet. Mounique's hands were still filthy. None of the children, or their families for that matter, believed in toilet paper. But they were making progress. They could count now both in Arabic and in French, the official language of the government. I was barely ahead of them, in my fractured Tunisian accent but they accepted me. I needed that. It was good to be back. Whom was I kidding? I had to come back. To put my father's death behind me for now, just like that. Go on, work here, and honor him in this way in the Peace Corps. He would have loved being a Volunteer himself, since it was he who suggested the idea to me, if he had not been saddled with five other children, a mound of debt and a second wife who needed lots of attention.

"Enna bared itay srir ou smene. Yiddy alisari fummi alimene." The day ended with a group song after the children assembled for pick-up by their mothers. "I'm a little tea pot short and stout, here is my handle, here is my spout…." In every song with the children, I faked guitar back up while fantasizing I was a lead vocalist in a rock band at some great outdoor concert in the States which I had sadly been denied attending while overseas. I loved the fact those little kids thought I had the greatest voice in the world.

The round iron rings in each of the mouths of the wooden lions' faces clanked against the hard wood as I unlocked the massive front door. The house was not locked and constantly cleaned while I was away. I couldn't I lock the house anyway, since I lived in four rooms surrounding an open courtyard. Kids ran along the roof constantly watching the Peace Corps Lady prepare breakfast or dinner. The bend over traditional Turkish-style toilet tucked in beside the kitchen lacked a door and was practically public to the eye from dawn to twilight. .

I came home just after dark to a welcome privacy. The total darkness was an adjustment after the glare of the gas lights in the street. The first thing I noticed was the makeshift Christmas tree I and others had made out of clumped-together olive branches with painted yogurt cups for ornaments. Then I remembered canceling the Christmas party we had planned right before the call because I would be travelling with Alan. Looking around, I realized that in my absence the cleaning lady had been so avid, I could now barely find my own things in my own space.

Because I really hadn't slept in the last forty-eight hours, I decided to just get into bed with most of my clothes on. This was customary for me because I never knew who would be on the roof watching Peace Corps Lady undress on any given night. I snuffed out the candle and put it on the stone floor beside the bed. I was so tired I wouldn't even hear the scratching of scorpions as they crawled across the pavement in the courtyard that night or the wail of the Arab imam early in the morning.

I flopped down on the heavy straw mattress nestled into the bedroom wall. The bed was so high I regularly used a ladder to climb up into it. It was so dark that without the candle I didn't see the unread mail fall off the bed onto the floor, but I heard it. It was only eight o'clock, even though it was pitch black outside. I lumbered back down the ladder, relit the candle, picked up the mail accumulated while I was gone and climbed back up in bed. Among the mail were two letters from the States. I opened the first one, which was post marked Boston, December 22, 1967 from my step-mother. "Ding Dong the Wicked Witch is dead!" rang the song of the Munchkins loud and clear in my ears at the thought of her.

Dearest Diana,

This is the fifth time I've written this letter. Surely it is the most difficult one of my life and I don't feel confident in my ability to generate the feelings in me that must be inside you.

Dad is VERY Sick. He sleeps 99% of the time. He has been in the hospital since the 15th. During his last week at home I said to him (which I had said often), "I think I'll write Diana and tell her what a lousy time you're having." He was adamant, as he has been right along, that I do no such thing. He has been so pleased with your Peace Corps progress and felt you really had landed on your feet (until you wrote about the college catalogues!). He has been terrified you would come home and genuinely did NOT want you to. I went to see Rev. Walke yesterday who told me that I should now write this in spite of Dad's wishes, so I am. Mr. W., too, feels very strongly you should NOT come home. Dad recognizes no one, so it would serve no purpose at all. Please believe me, Diana.

There are just no euphemisms to incorporate in a letter like this. You and I have been through quite a lot together and I don't need to tell you how I feel. Strange though it may seem, I love to think of you happy, active and learning and it must be so rewarding. Best news of all is your architect beau. He sounds almost good enough for you and I hope sensitivity is his long suit so that solace and diversion both will be available to you.

Trite and peculiar though it may sound to you—please after you have read this, gulped and digested this letter go outside, breathe deeply and thank God for everything positive you can think of. I do this about ten times a day and for some reason it really helps.

Hope your CARE pkgs. arrived-also the cheque (sic.) from Judy. Anne Chandler Tilson arrived in Tunis on the 16th and they would love to see you whenever you get there.

I will be in constant touch with you. Again, I reiterate, do not come home. If you would like to call, collect, once (I can't afford it any more) do so—10 p.m. is the best time. It may be that the PC will let you do so, on them!

Lots and lots of love, Diana. So many people could have written this so much better and for this I am sorry.

Joan

You can say that again. In some ways it was a good letter, but it failed to make me feel better about my stepmother. I remembered that time in my parents' room when I found the letter my stepmother wrote but never sent me. It began: "Honestly, sometimes I think, if your behavior doesn't change, you will be as crazy as your mother." It went downhill from there to address my lies and erratic behavior. What did she expect? The secretary had lured my father from his office and from my softball games into marriage. I just kept tying my shoes, over and over again, in knots in so

many ways to keep everything inside. I never let her know I saw the letter. And I never forgave her. Not then, and I would not now.

After I read the letter, I remembered the dream, the recurring dream that began in the summer after the concert in Tunis, six months before the overseas phone operator informed me through the static that my father had died the day before on Christmas morning.

The concert was a one night show by the great Louis Armstrong in a Roman amphitheater in Tunis. Louis Armstrong was my father's favorite singer. My father would sing along off key to his music at night: "Oh, the shark has pearly teeth dear and he keeps them out of sight." As Louis sang, my father's face floated in front of me and I felt his presence, even though he was half a world away. That night was the first of many nights of the dream.

In the dream members of my training group in Boston stood on the curb outside our dorm waiting to get on the yellow bus that would take us to the airport for the flight to New York en route to Tunis. My father had taken the morning off just to come say good bye. It was mild winter still. No snow yet, even though it was February.

The gray herring bone coat hugged his rugged frame over his pinstriped Brooks Brothers suit, his blue uniform. The collar of the coat was pulled up next to his pointy ears, his only physical imperfection. They stuck out like Howdy Doody's and everyone said so. He could make them wiggle like crazy. My father was Paul Newman gorgeous beyond belief. I idolized him. Where others found fault, I felt only fondness.

George Roberts was the healthiest, handsomest man who ever lived. Although he was sickly as a child, as an adult he never missed a day of work or play because of illness. He certainly never missed a golf game. After all, he had been an eleven-letter athlete in college. Maybe he drank a little too much, but that was part of his genuine interest in being in the middle of those around him. He loved and was loved by many. As they say, he never met a stranger. He was not the dying kind.

He smelled of Lucky Strikes, apple pie for lunch and Bay Rum. He was all man-father to me then and I wanted him all to myself. My stepmother, Joan, wanted him all to herself. But right now he was mine. We stood there on the curb together smiling at each other, talking with the other women, who, like me, were barely twenty-one and really were just girls.

21

On the sidewalk my father was waving to me. The right hand crossed his face and then his heart, then it lifted back up into the air above his head and out toward me. The motion repeated over and over. He was smiling, singing that Louis Armstrong tune. He was tapping his finger into the air imitating Louis' scratchy staccato pitch singing: "Oh, the shark has pearly teeth dear and he keeps them out of sight." And then I would wake up.

I watched the candle flicker to low and saw the wax oozing down over the empty wine bottle spout onto the bedside table. It hardened quickly into layers of dried stiff wax. Just like my heart. I needed to sleep but instead found an oil lamp and a fresh wick to light.

The second letter had been posted from New York City sometime after New Year's Day. It was from my mother, my "crazy" mother, dated January 22, 1968.

Diana, my darling,

What dreadful news for you, my little baby—and how brave you must have to be to be able to take it way over there.

My own impression is that your father was murdered. It was another one of those plotted, planned things—to accomplish for the secretary whatever she wanted as she had used him to serve her own purposes all along. She is some ambitious, criminally insane person from the lower classes and you all would be well rid of her.

Now, of course, you and Teddy and Cameron, your little brother, and I must be reunited. However, I leave it up to your own decision as to how you want to work this out.

I have complete confidence in you, my darling, to make all the decisions as to what you want us all to do. Take plenty of time to think and feel before coming to any conclusions.

I have not talked to Teddy and I have not written him either yet. I want to give him a chance for this to sink in before contacting him and talking to him in any way

at all.

Well, my darling—I love you my little baby—and we must not feel sad. I have many memories—but I don't want to cry. (As I'm saying this, tears are running down my face!)

Now, just relax. Take it easy. Don't rush. We have all been through the hell of this terrible marriage of his to Joan. We were made complete victims of their purposes. I feel your father George was a victim, too. Joan must be something too terrible!

Goodnight, my little baby. Will write very soon, my precious little angel.

Your Mother

Some kind of crazy. For the first time since the death, I could feel the pain flowing into my veins like the slow drip from an IV, arousing feelings, not tranquilizing them. My mother made sense to me in her own way. We both hated the woman who had come between my father and Markie and me. The oil lamp was flickering low but it didn't matter. High overhead the stars shone down brightly on the open courtyard. With the streaking light from the sky I could see many things clearly now on that night.

Meeting the Big Guy

My Peace Corps duty concluded in August, 1968. It probably wasn't a smart idea to fly into Washington, D.C. in the middle of violent demonstrations on downtown K Street near the Peace Corps office. Most of the glass in the storefronts had been smashed by the time I arrived. The protests were about racial discrimination, the broken glass allowed looters chasing booty into the empty shops.

Even before arriving home, while I was still in Tunisia, the Washington Headquarters had hired me as a recruiter for the Peace Corps in the Midwest territory. That meant travel to places like Spear Fish, South Dakota to recruit farmers to serve in India, or Bowling Green, Ohio, to find future TOEFL teachers (Teaching of English as a Foreign Language) for Tunisia. And to Des Moines, Iowa where I would meet my future husband, John. He would later become a conscientious objector doing his two year alternative service to his country as civilian counselor for dissident GI's in the military on the forty-four American bases in Japan during the Vietnam War.

I was full of national pride as a returning Peace Corps Volunteer coming home from Sousse, Tunisia, where I had served for the last two years. I had built and run a *jardin d'enfants*, a day care center, in the middle of a cemetery that had been bombed out during World War II. I was the living epitome of the well- known TV ad for the Peace Corps. The Peace Corps was a volunteer opportunity tailor made for those who saw the glass half full instead of half empty. At this point it felt like my glass was overflowing. I had never been so happy.

Back home in Boston before I left the country, the Boston Herald ran a story about me with the headline: Debutante Volunteers for Peace Corps Service in Africa. Later on, maybe because of my debutante history, the Peace Corps public relations folks picked me to be the 25,000th outstanding return Volunteer. It seemed a PR move to have the society ladies exhibit social service tendencies.

Right off the plane in D.C., I met with a reporter from the Washington

Star and did my first talk show interview. During it I was asked if I joined other PCV's in marijuana parties as had been reported about Volunteers in several African Countries and in India. "Well sir, if there were any drugs nearby I never saw them. I worked with 70 little kids in a two-room day care center, and I don't think they had much access to what you are asking me about." *Right answer.* Even the interviewer thought that was funny and quick.

Then I got to meet the big guy, President Johnson.

"How do you do, young lady, thank you for your volunteer service to your country. Every young person like you should take time to help others in some capacity, whether overseas, or right here in this country in Vista. Your father must be very proud of you."

"My father died last year while I was stationed in Sousse. I didn't get a chance to say goodbye but I did fly home to Boston for his service."

"I am so sorry to hear that. Most PCVs who come home on compassionate leave for a loved one do not return to the host country. You are a very brave woman, and I commend you."

"Hardly, brave, Mr. President, but thank you for your kind words."

This was my first inkling that even the highest dignitaries in the land may not be well prepared for even the smallest of audiences. I was embarrassed to have to tell the president of the United States that my father had passed away. Thank God he did not ask about my mother.

Another interview took place at what may have been the studio of an NPR stations in its early days-again that interest in the drug life of Peace Corps Volunteers.

Steve, the public affairs guy from the Peace Corps Washington headquarters went with me to the station. On the way he asked a lot of questions. How many children in my day care center? Did I have regular contact with the municipality? *Yes, I thought but did not say, too frequently, remembering the time the mayor asked me to have an affair.* Did I work with the Peace Corps architects to build the day care center? *Yes, and, I wondered if he actually already knew from the files that I lived with one for most of the time I was in Sousse.*

Just before we went on the air, Steve squeezed my arm and drew me close to him: "Now if you did a lot of dope over there, I don't want to hear about it. Just don't blow us out of the water with some statement about how mind blowing the drug experience was. Got it?"

Got it? Clearly I didn't get it, yet here it was again. I had been away so long I did not know what had already been happening in the States for much of the last two years. Drugs and experimental psychology had become a part of an American cultural current in which I had not participated. I did not yet know who Timothy Leary was and had not heard of those psychedelic mushrooms in the psilocybin project at Harvard. I did not know the catchphrases he popularized that promoted his philosophy. "Turn on, tune in, drop out", "set and setting", "think for yourself and question authority" were not in my vocabulary in English, Arabic or French.

Nor did I know about Ken Kesey who was out there on the West Coast celebrating drugs with music-and-light shows featuring a house band that evolved into the Grateful Dead. I was still listening to Simon and Garfunkel's first album. I had yet to experience Janis Joplin, Joan Collins, Joni Mitchell and the Whole Earth Catalogue.

"Miss Roberts, you have been honored by the President as an outstanding Peace Corps Volunteer. Why do you think you were chosen?"

Again I chose my words carefully: "I was very lucky to do more than teach English, my own language, like so many other volunteers. I was chosen to work with young children because I had been a baby sitter throughout most of my years in high school and beyond. I already spoke excellent French to be able to work with the officials in Tunisia but had to learn to speak to the children in their native language of Tunisian Arabic. I was able to completely immerse myself in Tunisian life. To build the *jardin d'enfants,* the day care center, to hire staff and enroll mostly poor little kids and their parents who spoke only Arabic was a tall order. But it worked. I loved every minute of the experience and I would wish it on anyone up for the challenge."

"Great interview, Miss Roberts. Good luck on your next adventure" the reporter smiled as he turned off the microphone.

I would soon be covering the Midwest, a place that would prove as culturally new to me as my first days on the foreign soil of Tunisia.

As it turned out, I would spend the next several years in Des Moines, Iowa. During a trip to Des Moines to recruit volunteers at Drake University, I met John Hodges, a young lawyer recently drafted out of the Peace Corps

while serving in Bolivia. Although he had gone into the Peace Corps knowing his status was 1A and that he was likely to be drafted, he was in a legal battle to protest the timing of his drafting from Bolivia. He was also morally opposed the Vietnam War or any other on. He had recently lost his court case in Des Moines and, and if he lost the subsequent appeal, would be sentenced to four years in prison as a felon for draft resistance. I soon feel in love with the man who was headed to becoming a felon.

John and I were introduced by John's roommate Wayne Wagner who was a fellow Peace Corps recruiter. We travelled the Midwest together. Wayne kept and apartment in Des Moines which he shared with John. When we travelled to Des Moines to speak at Drake University we scheduled a stay there to save money on the Peace Corps budget. I was not well prepared to use the toilet and tub, both of which were in the middle of the kitchen. No matter, I had experienced worse in the *marabout* in Tunisia.

That first night we went dancing. I was so taken with John that I never noticed that he had two left feet. The soft rock music and just being around him were all I needed.

Initially attracted to John's all American Midwest, football player good looks, I was soon even more impressed by his moral stance against war. I will admit to being much taken with the media coverage of John's case and the drama and excitement of being a part of it all. Joan Baez and her husband David Harris became my heroes. Later I would come to realize I was more probably more interested in adventure than in the activism of the time.

We got together and rented a house on 10th Street with some other returned volunteers and one Vista worker. It became the commune we called "HOUSE." Three months later John and I were married in a hippy ceremony in Waterworks Park with a trumpet playing behind a tree and the local TV station filming Des Moines' first "hippie wedding." Because John's father was a pig farmer, the night before the wedding several members of the commune stayed up all night in the park roasting a pig on a spit with an apple in its mouth for the big celebration. After the wedding the newlyweds and friends returned to the commune where we feasted on roast pig and received lots of gifts, mostly various items of Tupperware.

I was so eager to get my college degree that I resigned my job as a Peace Corps recruiter and began classes at Drake in the summer before our wedding. In the fall of 1969 I became a fulltime student in communications studying historical speeches from Edmund Burke to Jerry Rubin and later Spiro Agnew.

Three years went by while we lived in the commune as various people came and went: the ex-Vista Volunteer named Richie who had no teeth; Tom, the returned PCV from the Philippines who kept telling me college was useless- that I should become a writer; Fred, the Drake student who became a heroin addict; and various short term visitors, often musicians passing through town.

I studied while John pursued his draft case and practiced law, mostly pro bono. When the case came up for appeal in the 8th Circuit Court in Saint Louis, the court ruled that if John would step forward into the military, legally he could apply to become a Conscientious Objector and avoid a prison sentence for evading the draft.

During this time I had not heard from Markie for two years since the letter commiserating about my father's death on Christmas, 1967, during my first year in Tunisia. Nor had I written to her.

Then in the fall of 1969, five years before my conscience would later force me to seek Markie out in New York, I received a letter that let me know what Markie had been up to.

Miss Diana B Roberts
310 7th Street
Des Moines, Iowa

Dear Ms. Roberts:

I write to you on behalf of your mother Lillian Mark Byron Roberts. She has been a patient here at the Binghamton State Hospital for almost three years now since September, 1967.

She appears to suffer from general schizophrenia with obsessive compulsive tendencies.

She speaks daily of her children, in particular her oldest child, Diana. She misses her children greatly and since no one comes to visit her, including any member of her family, I fear that she is receding from progress here.

Please respond to this letter as to when you may come visit her. As you may know, many of our resources are being redirected to newly created Community Health Centers. It may be that we may no longer be able to care for your mother in an institutional setting here in upstate New York.

Please take the time to respond to this correspondence. Thank you for your time and interest.

Sincerely,

Ronald D. Rossberg, MD., PhD.

Chief Psychiatrist

I put the letter down after quickly reading it just once and stashed it away with all the others, keeping them bound by the same red rubber band in the same brown shoe box I carried with me everywhere. Hearing about Markie put me in an unending state of consternation and guilt. On the one hand, I knew I should respond. On the other, I could not stand to revisit those "precious little baby" phrases or those accusations about my father. I wanted to stay as far away from her and her life as possible. Just thinking about her made my brain and my pen freeze up.

I did not respond to this communication. The mention of schizophrenia still really scared me and made me shut down at the thought of investigating how Markie was surviving. Besides, I was involved in more important things like protesting Vice President Spiro Agnew during his "nattering nabobs of negativity" speech in Des Moines and crowding into a VW bus heading toward Washington, D.C. in the fall for the huge Vietnam rally to protest the war.

As it turned out that trip to Washington transformed me into a real anti-war activist. John and I and four others left Des Moines early Friday morning in a lavender painted VW bus formerly been owned by a town florist. The flower shop's faded sign was still shone through the paint on both sides of the bus: Frannie's Florals. The bus driver was a former member of the commune named Dennis who had moved out to take up with another member of House named Thelma. They married one weekend but were back now to go east with us. The other three riders were students from my classes at Drake.

On the way to D.C., Dennis unexpectedly had a drug reaction to speed that we did not know he had taken, and we and had to pull into a truck stop. He recovered after several hours of walking around outside the bus, trips to the diner to get fluids and food, and rest. John took over the wheel while Dennis slept in the back. The rest of us took turns driving until we arrived in DC twenty hours later in time to see several hundred thousand people converged on Washington to protest the Vietnam War. It was midday Saturday, November 17, 1969.

The day was cold and clear. There were lots of busses lined up on streets. I don't remember where we parked the bus, but I did know the bus was also going to be our hotel. Once out of the bus, we walked with thousands of others to the foot of the Capitol.

Although troops were not in view, I could feel the presence of Army and Marine Corps men stationed behind columns in Federal buildings along our route. Two thousand metropolitan police were on duty for the march, and the Pentagon and the Justice Department were packed with paratroopers.

We missed the opening of the rally which was led by three drummers followed by eleven coffins containing the names of 40,000 war dead. Behind them, a man carried a three-hundred pound cross proclaiming that if Christ were alive he would impeach Richard Nixon.

Banners and placards were everywhere. Signs made references to Spiro Agnew and the Silent Majority. I could hear chants of "One, two, three four. Tricky Dick, stop the war!"

Performers and speakers alternated throughout the afternoon on the podium below the Washington Monument. It took a long time, maybe an hour but we made our way to the front of the crowd. Some people smoked marijuana, but drugs were not a big part of the event. George McGovern and Eugene McCarthy spoke movingly and urged us to be strong and of good courage in this struggle to end the war. When the cast of Hair began singing "The Age of Aquarius" while releasing a host of flying doves into the air above the crowd, I realized I would be more moved by the performers than the public officials.

The music ranged from works by the Cleveland Orchestra to Mitch Miller. Some people in the crowd began dancing to tunes played on the banjo by Earl Scruggs. Demonstrators joined Pete Seeger singing "All

we are saying is give peace a chance." I sang along with them and raised my hands in the peace sign for several minutes. All the great musicians of my own personal hit parade were there: Arlo Guthrie, Mary Travis of *Peter, Paul and Mary* and Leonard Bernstein and playwright Adolphe Green. Even Timothy Leary, whom I had only recently learned of, was on hand in a weird buckskin outfit looking more like Daniel Boone than a hippie. Somehow in the excitement of it all I lost my wallet and my last twenty bucks.

That night press reported that there were only 250,000 demonstrators there that day, but it was later proven that there were more than 500,000 on hand to declare their disgust for the administration's war on Vietnam. When I returned home I received a small package from DC. Someone had found my wallet in the street and had sent it back to me with a note scribbled inside: "Thanks for making the trip. We are going to end this thing yet. Keep the fight alive! P.S. By the way I am keeping the $20." I did not mind at all.

What I did not know at the time was that the inauguration of Richard Nixon in 1969 ushered in a new perspective on the mental health front in the U.S. Between 1970 and 1972, his Administration worked assiduously to scale back National Institutes of Mental Health (NIMH) programs, many of which had survived only because of a sympathetic Congress. By 1973, however, the Watergate scandal was occupying the attention of the White House, and mental health policy issues faded from view. Nixon's resignation in the summer of 1974 was welcomed by those concerned with mental health policy issues, if only because he was perceived as an opponent of any significant Federal role in shaping and financing services. In the months just preceding and following Nixon's resignation, Congress undertook a reassessment of the CMHC program. The result was the passage of a mental health law in mid-1975 over President Gerald Ford's veto. Yet this legislation— which expanded the role of CMHCs— never addressed the fundamental issue of providing for the basic human and medical needs of persons with severe mental illnesses.

Once she was let out of the state institution in 1970, Markie began moving around New York City briefly inhabiting a number of temporary residences. While other former patients were moving in large numbers into abandoned hotels in Chelsea and other parts of town, where they could actually form communities and advocate for each other, Markie was the ultimate loner, seeking to live by herself in one room apartments or hotel rooms in shady parts of town. The bed, the table, the dresser and the lamp in each of her one room flats were most often nailed to the wall or the floor for security purposes. It didn't matter. The only possessions Markie really cared about went with her everywhere in a big, black, fake leather bag: Kleenex, the tin foil she used to cover the knobs of her dresser, a can of talcum powder, brown bobby pins, birth certificates of her children, her old marriage licenses, packets of salt from restaurants, instant coffee, Kotex pads with the insides removed so that they were just pieces of gauze with no purpose, and several pairs of black gloves.

Once John became a Conscientious Objector and I had my diploma, we headed to Tokyo, where John would serve his CO Service as civilian counsel in military Courts Martials on behalf of the ACLU and the American Friends Service Committee, an arm of the Quaker faith. Just before going to the Far East I received a letter from Markie. My younger brother Teddy had been in touch with her and given her my address and an update on my life with John

> Miss. Diana Byron Roberts Hedges
> 1310 7th Street
> Des Moines, Iowa
>
> Diana, my darling:
>
> I am more thrilled than I can possibly tell you that you are graduating from college. How absolutely stupendous!!!! Darling, how could you do it?!!! I am more proud of you with each passing day. It's so fantastic. I had no desire to go to college and would never have attempted any such thing.
>
> I am distressed beyond words that you say you are going to Japan, you mustn't go. You must stay here in this country with Teddy and Cammy and me. Let your husband go without you.

I know you married that farmer lawyer out there in Iowa where you are finally going to college (I am so proud of you) and living in that commune (I am not so proud of that).

You said he became a Conscientious Objector to this Vietnam War and has to serve our country in an alternative way by serving GI dissidents in Military Courts Martials. Why? Why? Why? Why does that mean you have to go with him?

Darling, the pregnancy test was negative. It's been several weeks now that I am overdue. I have had nothing to do with any man since I was forty years old and I'm about to be 54 later this month on the 23rd.

This was a great big colored man who had evidently seen me someplace and decided to pick on me! As I was opening the front door with the key downstairs—he appeared suddenly beside me and pushed his way in. He had a long thin knife, over a foot long, which he held across my throat. He demanded cash first and then seemed hell bent on rape, as hard as that is to believe. If I would not do exactly what he forced me to do, he would turn the knife around, sticking the point into my throat. He forced me up the stairs to what must have been near the top of the building.

I had on eight layers of things in the lower section. This slowed him down a lot. But still he was determined. I had on two Kotexes and three pairs of pants. Then he pushed the other three layers up. I had on two outer skirts besides a slip. First forced me to put my mouth on it and then forced it in lower down. It was all very strange and hard to believe that anyone could be that interested in the rape of an old woman of fifty-three!

The following day I was taking a taxi and the driver happened to be a colored man. So I asked him whether he thought this man of his race was just about the rape of a woman—or was he particularly out to rape a "white" woman. He said to me that he thinks definitely he wanted a white woman. He said there are some white men that are that way about colored women. He said it's almost like a disease with them.

Well darling, I don't want to bore you with all of this, but I want you and your brothers, Teddy and Cammy, to know that I have had nothing to do with any man since I was forty years old—until this unfortunate experience which I suppose has added to my knowledge in the mental field. Strange as it may seem I know the man was not insane.

I do not go out with anyone and have not in all this time. Therefore the question of being involved does not come up, as I do not want it to. I made this decision the summer of my attempt to divorce your father a second time—after remarrying him—was becoming final.

Well, my darling, I love you with all my heart. And I want you, Teddy, Cammy and I all to be reunited. We must be, darling, and I hope you have had enough of this marriage now and will return home to your mother and brothers.

I will write again very soon. Please, won't you forgive me for not keeping my writing up? There is absolutely no excuse for it. Everything has been going along just the same with me. Nothing is very different at all. I have had financial troubles though because I don't have enough to live on from my disability checks, so this has kept me worried and has made it hard for me to keep my writing to you up.

I telephoned you recently and some young man in that commune of yours told me you weren't there at the time. It's seems that many young people live with you in that house in Des Moines.

Well, darling, I will say good night for now. You are in my thoughts every single second. Consider that I am right there with you holding your hand through college, darling, my precious little baby. Please come back to Cameron and Teddy and me. We need you, darling.

All my love,
Your mother

At the end of the letter there was a genealogy of sorts, a list of all Markie's "accomplishments" in heavy black ink:

> *Lillian Mark Byron Roberts (Mrs.)*
> *Nee Lillian Mark Byron (Hagerstown, MD.)*
> *Married and divorced, twice, your and your two brothers' father*
> *George French Roberts, Sr. (now deceased) of Milton, Massachusetts.*
> *Both marriages in New York City.*
> *First divorce, Nevada, 1950. Second divorce, Alabama, 1958*
> *First marriage Heavenly Rest Church, Episcopal, March 13, year?*
> *I became pregnant with you eight months after George and I were married.*
> *Our second marriage was at a Baptist minister's home.*

In the litany Markie never mentioned that she became pregnant with Cameron

before, not after, my father and she were briefly married for the second time.

Surviving Chairman Mao

Driving home from the Needham Deaconess hospital in the darkness of early morning on April 16, 2002, after Markie breathed her last breath around 2:30 a.m., gave me way too much time to think before the sun would steer my thoughts to the day. On the way I remembered my visit with Markie so long ago in New York in early summer, 1974.

John and I came home from Japan to New York in the fall of 1973. John was going to work for Legal Services in Brooklyn, and I was going to enter graduate school at Hunter College for the next two years. But within a year, life would change dramatically.

Our time together in Japan at the height of the Vietnam War was a seminal time for both of us in political education and lifelong choices. John was basically a committed socialist, whereas I was just plain adventurous but without his fervor for activism. He served dissidents on those U.S. Military bases in Japan. I had a job as assistant editor of the main Japanese English daily paper, the Yomiuri Shimbun, which in English means "read/sell." Maybe my parents' marriage had not worked out, but we seemed a good fit and I was intent on making ours work. Or so I thought. The bonds began to fray in Japan as we grew in different directions.

We lived in an upstairs apartment in the house of a Japanese family. The father was head of the treasury in Japan and had been educated in America at Harvard. The wife had gone to high school in Andover, Massachusetts. In our spare time, we amused our landlords by practicing their English playing games of Risk and Monopoly with them several nights a week and teaching them how to make different kinds of spaghetti. John spent many nights going to ex-patriot anti-Vietnam rallies and meeting with Japanese dissidents opposed to the presence of the Americans in their country.

One night we returned home from hearing a speech made by a US Congressman. It was the time of the Watergate hearings, and we had hoped he would give us some inside opinions on the proceedings.

"What did you think of the speaker," I started.

"He was okay."

"Okay? What do you mean?"

"He was okay. I had no problem with him."

I felt the adrenalin rising. These bland responses were becoming more frequent. I poured some sake and waited for John to expand his response.

Then I asked, "Would you like some more?"

"No thanks, I don't feel the need of it."

God damn it, talk to me, I thought. Why is every sentence a moral judgment? Of course you don't need it. But I need you, your pulse or some more description of your thoughts other than, okay, good, fair or poor. I don't need to live with a number three on a scale of five utterances per day. Screw you. No, screw me. Please!

"Let's go to bed." I lit another cigarette in defiance of the silence. "If you want to make love, I'll get out the futon." I thought I had really offered him a choice.

"I'd feel a lot better if you were less aggressive, Diana."

I quickly moved away in the direction of the radio to hear The Stars and Stripes broadcasting a replay of the day's Watergate hearings with the stentorian Sam Ervin sending us Shakespearian quotes over the airwaves during his inquiries. I tried to read my book on sexual politics. Later, I heard the beginnings of Fibber and McGee reruns coming over the airwaves as I fell asleep. They were such a compatible couple.

The first three years of our marriage had been full and good. So full, in fact, that living in the commune with other PCVs and human rights workers opposed to the Vietnam Way left us little time to get to know each other outside the group. Now we seemed to know each other no better.

John and I had moved to Japan initially as a way to escape the cynicism that the Vietnam War was creating in our lives in America. We thought we would feel more at home among other dissidents abroad who were a part of the great New Left, intellectuals disaffected after earlier being named in the early 60's as JFK's the best and the brightest.

I found that I was more than just a foreigner in Japan. I became foreign to myself. It was the first time John and I had to face each other alone. No commune. No comrades. No common ground. Only the Armed forces radio blaring at us over the tatami mats.

I longed for John to talk less of Chairman Mao over dinner and more of me, of the stuff of why we were together in this fight for social change.

We were so equal I could hardly breathe for wishing we didn't divide all tasks right down the middle. John cooked three and a half times a week and I did the same. I made a lot of money. He promised to take me around the world when the struggle to end the war was over. I would pay for it and was saving for the air fare by working a sixty-hour week in addition to teaching English to members of the Japanese Treasury Department. I was having fun teaching guys to use knives and forks Western style when they would go to meetings in Geneva. I would tell them about life in America. At home, increasingly, I was living with a stranger.

When I almost, but didn't, have an affair with an American ABC television reporter stationed in Tokyo, I knew things might ultimately come undone when we came home to America. I even made the mistake of telling John about this almost mishap. He seemed to have little reaction, except to say, "You must do what you choose to do."

We returned to the United States in September of 1973 just in time for me to start graduate school in New York City at Hunter College. We spent a lackluster Christmas with John's parents on their farm in Iowa. I felt myself becoming more and more restless and less interested in John on many levels. When we would go to the movies, I would fall asleep as a defense against having to be engaged in conversation or commentary.

By the early summer of 1974, I had dropped out of graduate school, was getting divorced and was living a nomadic existence in New York. By day, I worked alongside other eager young staffers, both Republicans and Democrats, in Nelson Rockefeller's office on the 23rd floor at Rockefeller Center. By night I partied with those who shared a house with me in the Hamptons on weekends. I had recurring fears about the note I found in my stepmother's drawer when I was fifteen that stated plainly her belief I might well follow in the path of my mother to an unbalanced state. Now I had to prove to myself that prediction untrue.

In A New York State of Mind

By the time I turned thirty, was married and now divorced, I had not seen Markie since I was sixteen, except once for lunch. But now, in 1974, I had to see her again, not just because she asked to see her "precious angel baby" but because I needed to for my own state of mind. Too many images of her had filled my nightly canvass of dreams as an adolescent: Chagall-like paintings of Markie and me danced before my eyes, of each of us dangling from a noose in the sky that came from nowhere before heavy black objects like meteors fell on us. I had to find where the noose came from and why. For once and for all I had to come face to face with Markie, to understand her history and to know that I was not destined to be the crazy person she was.

To be truthful, once I felt divorce might be in my future, things began slowly coming apart around me. I would lose my keys or forget to show up for class on time. I was tempted to have an affair with the professor for whom I was a teaching assistant. And my thyroid was out of whack causing me mood swings that made me ride a high and low all in one day. Was I going crazy? Luckily, I found a German psychiatrist on the Upper East Side who was willing to see me for a reduced price because she "liked women's cases" and was quite the feminist.

It took only two sessions for Dr. Haas to come up with a verdict in her thick German accent. "My dear, you are a fine young woman who is experiencing all the confusing but natural repercussions of going through a divorce. You forget your keys because you no longer want to be responsible in this situation; you want someone else to take over the management of your life. I suspect the stress is affecting your thyroid adversely. You must see a doctor for your glands, but I can tell you your sanity is very much intact. If you were going to experience the schizophrenia described in the case of your mother, it would have happened long ago, as it did in her mid-teens."

Phew. Finally there was a reassuring diagnosis by an impartial judge. It wasn't a home run, but I felt safe on base for the first time.

A sticky spray of rain was covering the city. I pressed my hand discreetly against my skirt in a vague attempt to adjust my dampening panty hose and waited for the light to change. Heading up Madison Avenue toward 59 East 79th to my grandmother Muffy's apartment in the hot June rain was becoming a real challenge on foot.

"Lady, you planning to take a boat or are you gonna cross the street?"
"Sorry, officer. Yes. Thanks for holding the traffic for me."

My pulse quickened at about 60th Street as I watched the warm spray descending on the cars moving slowly uptown like an electronic cattle herd. My steps kept pace with the speed of a bus trapped on all sides by barely moving cars with fogbound windows. Only the taxis in New York ever have it easy. They know how to get in and out of everywhere fast, a talent I was only beginning to learn to appreciate.

I felt queasy and the smell of the streets that mixed with my sweaty anticipation didn't help. The rain and the scent of a nearby dog's warm urine mingled in the air and invaded my nostrils as I approached East79th Street. It was the smell of dog and pee I knew from years before as a small child of three living in New York's Greenwich Village. Those were the days when I would walk together with my father. We would pass our neighbors walking their dogs. Dad would smile and wave to each one, all the while proudly showing off his first child.

Everyone has his or her own gimmick for trying to feel safe when they are scared. Me, I try to lose my fear by making myself become the inanimate things around me at the time. As I moved up Madison Avenue, I became an umbrella in a sea of umbrellas marching along beside me. I never actually owned one, so I could feel the rain mist landing on my eyelashes, making it difficult to see up the long blocks toward my destination. Nevertheless, the umbrella thing was working for me. Wet or dry, I was feeling a little more at ease inside my skin.

I moved across Madison turning right onto 79th, which brought me almost full stop at my destination, my grandmother Muffy's first floor apartment at 59 East 79th Street. I slowed my pace on the last full steps that brought me face to face with my past.

The first thing that came into view from a block away were the salmon pink window shades, scalloped at the edges with the bottoms trimmed

in torn beige tassels of uneven lengths. They stretched down over the two front windows of the first floor apartment creating a façade of faded grandeur for passersby. Seeing those windows, I instantly became six years old again remembering all the times we stayed there with Muffy and Markie when Markie was not herself. The windows suddenly became enormous, and I became small and compliant and helpless all over again.

From just a half a block away, I caught sight of my mother standing in the doorway next to the window with salmon pink shades, covering her eyes with her rail thin gloved right arm to protect her face from the summer rain outside. Her face on that day, as on every day that I remember, was covered in thick white talcum powder. She had never lost the belief that it would protect her face from all kinds of uncleanliness. The black wool gloves were a part of her uniform. She didn't like to touch anything because of the possibility of germs. Even from a distance I could feel her eyes darting in uncertainty, waiting, just waiting for me.

Instinctively, I took a long moment to protect myself from this woman whom so often I had relegated to the past. Until now she had been in a safe place in my mind. She was an ancient snapshot in my wallet. She was a photograph on my desk: a thirteen-year-old in high leather boots and jodhpurs with no concerns except how to smile at the photographer. This visit was not going to be like that. It was going to be visceral and messy. It wasn't really even going to be about my mother.

The funny thing about my mother is we never called her "Mother" or "Mommy" or "Mama." My mother was actually named Lillian Mark Byron and called "Little Mark" or "Markie" because her mother's first name was also Lillian: Lillian Mark Crawford Byron. Lillian Mark became "Muffy" and Little Mark became "Markie." To my two brothers and me, our mother was always just "Markie," never something more maternal.

My thoughts forced their way back to the present, and I realized I had to hasten my steps up that last half block to the doorway where Markie stood. I glanced at the newsprint staring up at me from the stand on the corner and mused on the fact that Nelson Rockefeller would soon become Gerald Ford's running mate. Everything was about to change.

I swallowed hard and before I realized it, I shouted, or rather squawked, "Hello." In contrast to my stiff, loud, dry rasp, Markie made no sound at all as I approached her.

Markie reached down, simply, with one clean movement, drawing me to her thin flat-chested body. The embrace was genuine, firm, like a long awaited drink of water in which there is no time for breaths, only great gulps with the water spilling out over the edges of your mouth down all over your body. I noticed a small amount of talcum powder had rubbed off Markie's face onto my shoulder. The imprint of the powder would stay with me later, along with the demonstration of her unbridled affection.

"Why, Diana, you look marvelous! How good of you to come. I have been waiting such a long time to see you." I had not remembered how much like a genuine New York aristocrat she sounded, the words like honey, the syllables selectively uttered, resonating together perfectly into thoughtfully chosen superlatives.

It had been five years since had I heard from those doctors in that state hospital, their communiques, stark white letters, that yellowed with age as I kept them stored a safe place. All those letters from her on my desk, any desk where I happened to be, would reach me. "Dear Diana, Dear Precious Baby Angel, Dear Oldest Child by your father George whom I married in our first marriage before my commitment and then again the second time after the birth of your youngest brother whom we called Cameron..." I tried not to read them. But the albatross was always with me making me anxious and uneasy, but never compelling enough to make me respond.

Didn't my mother know I was now way past "Precious Baby Angel"? Didn't she know I was past thirty by now? That I had really grown up?

I entered the dark, cool front hall of 59 East 79th Street. Markie opened the door to the apartment and to my former life. When I was six we moved from the Village here to the apartment just above Muffy's so that I could go to the Rudolph Steiner School, it turned out, for just one year. We spent a lot of time in Muffy's first floor apartment, especially as Markie mothering skills began to fade. My parents had divorced the year before and my Dad had taken a job far away in Texas in a company that was making munitions for the Korean War.

At the end of the school year, in early summer, Markie was gone and we were not told why or where she went. I would find myself in Texas with my father and younger brother Teddy not remembering how we got there. Now in a way I was coming home to a place I knew well but only briefly.

The living room and single bedroom, still all salmon and sallow, seemed much smaller to me now that I was fully grown.

Markie began with that artificial, formal tone, as if I had never met Muffy before. "Diana, you remember Muffy, my mother, your grandmother. This is your maternal grandmother, wife of your grandfather, Edward J. Byron, no relation to your father's family."

I thought of those letters again, the ones with all the family names. I never could stand it while I lived with her or whenever Markie started talking like all the "begats" in the Book of Genesis. It set up too much distance. This time, if I tried to get close, regain some of those missing years, would she back off into a litany of names and dates of people the way her letters did, always writing about people I was actually related to, often calling them, "murderers," "thieves" and "whores." Even, Dad, who supposedly "slept with diamond ringed black prostitutes," was no longer alive to defend himself from her verbal onslaughts.

I sat down squarely on the pale green silk Empire couch that doubled as a bed for Markie when she stayed with Muffy. Oh, God, not this, not so soon. Please don't talk that way now. I crossed my legs and asked for an ashtray. Muffy at least seemed content to remain quiet and begged off to take her afternoon beauty nap.

"You look wonderful, Diana!" my mother exclaimed. "How long has it been? I remember our last meeting in the train station in Boston before you left for Africa. Back Bay wasn't it? With your brother? We ate lunch at the Red Coach Grille. I was afraid you would marry a black man, or worse, an Arab. But you survived and came home to me. You were such a beautiful child, and you have become a beautiful woman. I am so proud of you. I've followed everything you have done."

Not everything, not really anything. What about all those years when you should have been there? Was it better or worse for me that you couldn't be there?

But maybe this wasn't going to be so bad. I had forgotten the open affection, the complete love for a child she had but never had the capacity to care for except to adore from afar. No doubt about it, she was, in her own way, my best supporter to date, as she was at those rare times in my early life before she and my Dad divorced, when she would praise me as her precious one and talk to me intimately with little confidences. She made me feel loved by being herself a child with me at those times. I knew I could not deny that some praise was due this woman, half mother, half child. Yet fully mad.

"My precious Little Everything. You didn't think about sleeping with nor marrying an African black man, did you? From the Peace Corps? Or was there a Japanese man when you were in Japan? You know your father liked strange, exotic women, especially blacks. All colors. He liked to give them things to wear. But you're not like him. Tell me you are not like him." Markie moved the ashtray on the coffee table closer to me. Was this simply good manners or was she making a gesture to reach out to me?

She started right in. "Your father was a most difficult man." *Not this again.* "He loved people and parties around him, but he could never hold a job. There I was in the apartment here in New York, day in and day out, with two small children to feed and no manner of means. I never really loved him, you know. It was really the other boy. We were going to marry. I told him to write me. When the letter came, it was already too late. I was engaged to your father. I was already twenty-six and my parents thought it was time."

I felt the strain and tiredness closing in on me, but I fought off those enervating demons by taking time out to photograph mentally the woman who brought me into this world and then left me to fend for myself.

Markie switched topics and mentioned that the few things she had bought came "exclusively" from the Irvington House Thrift Shop in New York. It was easy to see Markie had been a long time faithful customer of this second hand repository of clothes once worn by Junior Leaguers, at least twice, before they were discarded for charity. On this day, Markie was literally wrapped in the combined cast-offs of every fashion era prior to, and including, the mid 1970's.

With something like pride, Markie sported a blue jean jacket with hippie-like spiders sewn into the jacket over the right shoulder in red and yellow. It easily could have been worn on stage originally by a member of the cast of "Hair." Black wool Capri slacks hugged her thin thighs to meet white bobby socks on top of black Capezio flats. If Markie were not in her mid-sixties, she could have been mistaken for any trim teenager weighing 125 pounds and ready to boogie. Lots of manic energy there.

Underneath the jacket were not one but three black sweaters, each layer heavier than the one beneath. Two strands of oyster colored poppet beads hung from her neck over the outermost turtleneck sweater. Even in the heat of the apartment, Markie seemed to shiver, her body not in tune with the reality of the heat surrounding her. She was tiny. Even in all those sweaters she looked small and thin. Markie claimed she was five feet seven, but it was obvious shock treatments, poor eating habits and a few missing teeth meant that she hadn't taken good care of herself in the last few decades.

The crowning glory of this "fashionista" was Markie's signature hat. Perched on her head, brim turned up, was a very cocky baseball cap with a large white NY for New York Yankees emblazoned on the top of the cap squarely in the middle. Her whole coif was held together tightly with brown bobby pins above her oval shaped face. She had the habit of covering it with white talcum powder to make her eyes appear deeper set in her oval shaped face. Maybe it was just a mask, a way to set herself apart from others. The milky white kabuki face was familiar to the neighbors as she wandered the Upper East Side of New York daily carrying all her belongings with her in a giant black fake leather bag large enough to carry a bowling ball. At night she would return to sleep on the sofa in Muffy's apartment at 59 East 79th Street.

I decided we should go out for some lunch. We went to a nearby deli and slid into seats way in the back where it was dark enough so no one not to really notice us. This turned out to be a good thing.

I ordered a salad because even back then I was always dieting. Markie ordered a hamburger after asking the waitress if there were any sugar in the bun.

"We don't put sugar on our hamburgers, M'am," the waitress stated flatly, acting like everyone knew that.

"I mean do the buns get made with sugar in them? I do not eat sugar."

"I will check, M'am, but I doubt it. Did you say a cheeseburger with fries?"

"No cheese. I don't eat dairy products."

Markie was growing anxious. She began rubbing her hands over and over and reached into the black bag for a Kleenex to wipe her hands free from any dirt in the air.

The salad and the burger arrived quickly. Markie removed the bun from the burger because she was sure the bun was "tainted" with sugar.

She then claimed I shouldn't eat the lettuce in my salad because it had been sprayed with pesticides. She said she knew this from the course she had taken in Lake Champlain while Dad was in the Navy. She continued with her proclamations about Kotex insisting I should remove the innermost pad because it contained toxic chemicals. I was beginning to feel sick and less than hungry.

Before Markie raised the burger to her mouth, she started to sprinkle salt over the meat. The salt ran down out of the shaker onto the burger until half of the burger was covered in white and the salt shaker was empty. She proceeded to the next booth and brought back another shaker. The second shaker, originally full, was completely emptied. There was now a mound of "snow" on the burger on the plate next to the discarded bun. Markie pushed her fingers around in the salt, picked up the covered burger and bit off half of it in one large bite. Apparently, she could not taste the overwhelming salt. It seemed she also did not feel hot or cold in her three sweaters.

As Markie chewed and talked, I noticed that, but for the clothes, we really did look alike. Was that some kind of indication that there were other genetic similarities? Might I have the crazy gene?

"That was in my first commitment," she was saying. "In that private institution, a wonderful place in Massachusetts." And what about the other commitments? Six times in and out of hospitals. Manic, depressive, or schizophrenic? She could name all the dates and places of her commitments in the same manner as she could name all her relatives in letters and reel off the names and origins of the Greek Gods. While her mind was aberrant, her memory was photographic. If she were religious she probably could recite the book of Genesis by heart. How could she be so right about names and dates and places and so wrong about my dad? He was kind and gentle. She said he was a murderer. She claimed Dad was irresponsible with money, and that only she could properly care for me.

That's the thing about people who have been institutionalized. They are literally marginalized. They think in the "margins," the very specific margins, speaking parenthetically, classifying everything in words and on paper so as not to forget, so as not to be forgotten. *And so God made the world that we would not forget.* "And on the first day, in my first commitment…"

There was Markie doing the Genesis thing again. For Markie, the fear of being misidentified and losing identity in the maze of mental health bureaucracy had been too much. Markie was put in an institution because she had lost her sense of self. Did they really expect her to regain it in a place for the insane? She had known it all along and survived each commitment. That's why she spoke in a suffocating litany.

"The first time, I was only sixteen." She chattered on as I tried to finish my lunch. "It was Christmas of my junior year in school. They made me go to that place in Massachusetts for two weeks. But already I had begun to know all the things to say to get out of that place. Always identify yourself, your parents, your school, your siblings, when they were born and where. If you can identify, quantify and qualify, then you are not crazy. It's like the Greek Gods. I know all their names and their Latin names, too. Remember when I taught them to you?"

I paid the bill, and we returned to the apartment. At the end of an hour, Muffy woke up from her beauty nap to pursue her evening ritual of bath and beautification. She once owned a line of beauty products under the brand name of Zandra which she designed during her love affair with Mr. Bergdorf or Mr. Goodman. No one in the family remembers which. It seemed slightly bizarre that a woman of her age would primp so excessively to greet no one but us at the end of the day, but then she had been Zandra and I had not. Nor had my mother been. I wondered if that could have been why things began to go wrong for Markie in the beginning. Was it from neglect when her mother, divorced in Markie's teens, was forced to go to work fulltime at Bonwit Teller's selling wedding dresses?

In another thirty minutes Muffy reappeared silently, seeming almost docile, to serve coffee to Markie and me, to touch up a few plants, and to draw the shades completely closed in the waning afternoon. A slow whistle crept into the sound of water perking in the tiny Pullman kitchen, which was separated from the living room by an ancient Chinese silk screen brought home from some furniture consignment shop.

I looked from my grandmother to my mother, to myself, to the three generations within me and to the thought of my own unborn children. What rogue misshapen genes might forecast their futures? How had my mother been both insane and sane, so uncaring and yet so loving? I wanted to know everything and not anything.

Markie had been institutionalized at sixteen in 1933 but then was fine until she began having children. Postpartum depression was not a concern when I was born but when it recurred a second time after the birth of my younger brother Teddy, we were sent to stay with our Dad in Texas. She would be put away a third time after the birth of Cameron. Each time it had to have been engineered by Muffy or my Dad, but I would never know. I had lost track of her commitments. Many people like her in New York and other places by the time I saw her had been deinstitutionalized and were out on the streets.

In that instant on that afternoon I felt and heard a voice within, low and soft, but steady and growing. Markie began to shrink in front of me, and in my eyes grew smaller and smaller until I knew one day she would become the child and I her unwilling parent. Had she been my unwilling parent? Or had her illness made her unable to make responsible choices?

That day, with my grandmother, we were three fragile females sealed together by blood and rain on a quiet summer afternoon in New York. Suddenly I was humming Simon and Garfunkel's *Hello, Darkness, My Old Friend*. I was ready to move on. I wanted to sing that kind of darkness out of my head. I sat there, numb to protect myself, and willed myself to become the Chinese screen for our last moments together before goodbyes. I was already late for my Junior League meeting just around the corner in Mrs. Astor's old house. The League had become my latest refuge from divorce and family. Our family has always had its own way of escaping things it could not handle.

"Hey, lady, my lucky day, I get to see you twice! I got pregnant women who move faster than you on their feet on the way to delivery room."

"If you're gonna cross, lady, move it already yet!"

As I looked back, Markie filled the whole doorway. She was smiling.

Her huge brown eyes sought to hold me in her sight for a little longer, but I was already crossing the street, moving away. I was both torn and compelled to leave Markie, and I reached somewhere back in my head for a song that could soothe my spirit:

> *Hello, darkness, my old friend,*
> *I've come to talk with you again,*

To lift my feeling of sadness I quickly switched to my favorite song: *slow down, you move too fast, you've got to make the morning last..........*

48

lookin' for life and feelin' groovy. Simon and Garfunkel were always there for me when I needed them, in the Peace Corps and again now as I was leaving my mother standing alone in the

doorway. As I sang to myself, mother and grandmother became a virtual Polaroid, freeze framed forever in my mind there in the apartment in New York on the Upper East Side. I thought this was meant to be a lasting goodbye.

Markie in the Mirror

On my dressing table at home, next to the silver hair brush and comb with my initials DBR, is a silver framed photo also with my initials that captures Markie at about age thirteen. The initials are a comfort to me as I imagine, perhaps falsely, that these things may have been given to me by my father as a reminder that my mother was once a healthy teenager in a wealthy and stable home.

Markie looks happy and confident seated for the photographer in her jodhpurs and high leather riding boots. She had been told since the day she was born that she was gorgeous, and in the photo she looks like she believed it. At the time she was a very pretty teenager. Her hair in the photo is shiny brown, cut in a smart pageboy, her luminous brown eyes peer out from beneath perfectly shaped eyebrows. She has the high cheekbones and oval-shaped face perfectly suited to the models of the day that she would later become. Like all of her younger siblings, she was born at the hands of a homeopathic doctor. Her mother Muffy took no drugs or painkillers in all her pregnancies in order for the children to be healthy and *perfect*.

You can imagine from the photo that Markie would soon turn heads as a young woman at coming-out parties in Baltimore and Boston. By the time she was thirteen she stood five feet seven with a well proportioned figure and dancer's legs. She had the style and look of an aspiring Greta Garbo. Her parents' lifestyle and resources allowed her to ride her own horse. She loved horses and early on preferred animals to people because, as she would later tell me, you could trust them. And like Jackie Kennedy to come, she had that wide vacant stare that made men gravitate to the mystery she exuded in public and in private.

For most of Markie's early childhood in Hagerstown, Maryland, the family leather tanning business was very successful. It allowed Markie's parents, Muffy and Edward, to have a house in France where Markie and her five younger siblings lived in the winter and a summer house in Dublin, New Hampshire. In 1926 the company decided to open a branch back in the Boston area and settled on Roxbury where young Edward would be stationed to work at the site. He and Muffy bought a house in nearby Milton and sought private schools for the growing family. At thirteen Markie entered Beaver County Day School for girls before being sent t age sixteen to board at Miss Hall's School for Girls in the Berkshire Hills of Western Massachusetts. She first met my father, George Roberts, on the front porch of the house at 108 Canton Avenue at age fourteen.

Due to changes in fashion and the advent of paved roads, leather and canvas leggings were dropped and shoes became the main product of the company by 1935. Fifteen years later in 1954, production was on the decline. Cannon Shoe Company purchased Hagerstown Shoe in 1968 and, in October 1984, citing competition from foreign imports, the factory closed its doors for good.

Muffy and Edward were, by any measure, an ambitious and stylish couple, but their spendthrift lifestyle, the 1929 stock market crash, a move from Boston back to expensive New York on the Upper East Side, and the decline of the business over time took a toll on their marriage. At one point, when Muffy's spending habits reached their peak, my grandfather was forced to take out an ad in the New York Times requesting that retail stores decline the purchases of one Mark C. Byron. In 1950, following their divorce, my grandfather moved back to Hagerstown to work for the company and later for Fairchild Aircraft until his death in 1968, the same year the company was sold. Muffy kept the second floor apartment at 59 East 79th and went to work in the wedding department of Bonwit Teller.

Whatever else she was, Muffy was definitely tough. She came from a middle class family. Her father, George Douglas Crawford, had been a doctor in Hagerstown. It was rumored that during one of his house visits in the surrounding towns he fathered a child whom he later supported. During World War I Muffy met her future husband, my grandfather Edward J. Byron, through family acquaintances. My mother, Markie their oldest child was born in 1917 the year before the war ended. Next in line there was my uncle Edward, known as Ted. Ted was kicked out of several private schools before joining the Air Force and ultimately met an untimely death flying his plane into a mountain in Italy. After Ted, came Margaret, who took early refuge from Muffy by marrying a man from Texas, with whom she bore nine children and ultimately died of alcoholism. Then came Don, the real estate developer, who married twice unhappily and in later life, before his death in his mid-seventies, became an ardent rightwing Republican.

Markie was to become many things to her own mother. At first she was a dream child, an anchor for Muffy's future and a first family heir. Later, but not too much later, she became an irritation, something Muffy could not control. And finally she became a long term imposition to her family, both physical and financial.

Markie was twelve when the stock market crashed. By 1936, when she arrived at the proper age for her to "come out" as a debutante, the family had lost considerable resources but not yet its social standing. Style section photos in newspapers of the day in both New York and Boston showed a glowing and vibrant Markie and noted that at age nineteen she had already become a successful model and performer in the Vincent Club cabarets in Boston.

As the product of a wealthy and somewhat protected upbringing, Markie suffered exposure to the economic downturn that may in part have contributed to Markie's first breakdown. Others it was caused by the often cruel oppression of her domineering mother.

Muffy became known as a big spender in those days and could be wildly extravagant at times. Though her modus operandi was somewhat risky, her objective was clear: she needed money to fund her extensive spending habits. She kept on unsuccessfully spending money to make money. In Muffy's defense, the 1930's were trying times for many, not just the socially minded Byrons.

In the Great Depression the American dream had become a nightmare. What was once the land of opportunity was now the land of desperation. What was once the land of hope and optimism had become the land of despair. Bing Crosby sang out over the air waves to the country "Brother, can you spare a dime?"

There was such instability in the country that the economic downturn of the period produced anxieties in many people on many levels. The exuberant post WWI decade was followed by huge unemployment, economic depression and droughts on farms in the Midwest. The ranks of the unemployed grew and the country shifted toward crisis. Dorothea Lange recorded the nation's slump in her photographs. And while the Byrons did not look like the skinny starved farmers who showed up in her

photos, the result for them was disaster of a different kind. Ultimately, along with their money, they lost their social status in all the places they inhabited.

There was a slow draining of their longstanding friends. One by one, families whom they used to spend summer days with fell out of their circle. The Byrons no longer went to France for the winter, not even during school vacations. They rented out the house in Dublin for half of each summer. But the Byrons were trained to hide their feelings. The same was true for Markie. In her lifetime she could never really come to grips with the fact that life her had changed forever. Instead, her only defense was to withdraw from the world.

The first time Markie exhibited signs of her future ill health she was home in Milton on vacation from Miss Hall's. George had already fallen hopelessly in love with her two years before, when he met her on her front porch while his parents were inside visiting the Byrons. Her aloofness was a stimulus to his ardor. The attraction for him was Markie's apparent coolness, her dark beauty and her quiet, restless energy always just below the surface. When attracted to his popularity and good looks others girls became too aggressive for George. He had no way to know that Markie had already begun the first of many escapes from the real world that so troubled her. That year after a week without sleep or food, Markie ended her vacation with two weeks of convalescence at Boston's preeminent mental health facility, McLean Hospital.

Markie recovered, graduated from Miss Hall's and came out as a debutante in both Boston and New York in 1936, in spite of the decline in family fortunes. Many years later I learned from my uncle that Markie's father casually told her that they were penniless in the limo on the way to Markie's debutante ball at the Boston Ritz.

Markie seemed unaware or unaccepting of her new circumstances. Perhaps Muffy helped to maintain a sense of denial by continuing to spend recklessly. Along with other debutantes of the day, Markie proceeded to join the Vincent Club, an exclusive ladies charitable organization in Boston that raised money for a local hospital every year by putting on musical theatricals for families and friends. She was shy but her quiet manner made her seem mysterious to her contemporaries. At eighteen having just graduated from Miss Hall's, she began a modeling career and became a Vincent Club show girl. Neither she nor her parents mentioned to anyone her stay at the mental hospital during the winter break of her junior year.

During this time, still in her teens, Markie began her one and only lifelong hobby of collecting teacups, demitasse teacups. In later years, this enduring habit led her to produce gifts of certain "unpurchased" items lifted from the shelves of the local Hadassah thrift shop or other consignment stores on New York's Upper East Side. Over the course of her lifetime Markie "collected" nearly two dozen demitasse cups that I have faithfully kept and still use on many occasions. Taken together, they are a silent testimony to Markie's attempt to preserve a remnant of the privileges of her early life. They form the legacy that Markie wanted more than anything to pass on to her children.

To be specific, the teacups that Markie shoplifted were not just regular teacups. They were demi-tasse cups, fragile and beautiful porcelain vessels from all over the world. Each cup and saucer had a story that Markie treasured. She gave me my first one when I was nine. It was a beautiful cup and saucer, hand decorated in thick gold paint with touches of pink on a crisp white porcelain background. The underside bears the mark "LS&S Limoges France," and was dated circa 1900. The Byrons no doubt acquired this particular cup and others when the family lived in France. There is a small speck on the rim where some gold paint has flaked off, but it is hardly noticeable. There are no chips or cracks or staining. Each looks as if it had never been used. This is how Markie would have liked her life to be: perfect, preserved like a tea cup, untouched and untarnished.

I have many others, twenty in all, some given to me by Markie and some I have collected to carry on in her memory, to keep a piece of her with me. There are two blue and gold Coalport demitasse cups I picked up in Harwich, England, both made at the turn of the nineteenth century, when bone china was in great demand and the Coalport Factory became the leading producer of enamel-painted flower decorated objects. There are cups from Dresden, Germany, one from a trip to Santa Fe, New Mexico, one from the William Morris Collection in England. The bottom of one cup, covered in coral and lavender daisies reads "Paragon, Bone China, by appointment." Another pale green and lavender cup and saucer painted with heavy gold flowers is labeled "made in occupied Japan." Each one is fragile, yet all have survived.

Markie knew that demitasse cups had been used by her family and families like hers for post prandial rituals or for high teas in the afternoon. To collect them made her feel young and special again. It made her feel a part of a genteel world no longer accessible to her.

All things, both inside and outside the family, combined to take their toll on Markie's mental health early in her life.

Ladies of the Vincent

The year was 1936 and the **Boston Herald** headline read: *Rehearsals at High Pitch for Annual Vincent Revue*. A subhead ran *"Tonight at Nine, a New Type of Production for Club Will Be Given with Audience Seated at Small Tables."* This headline was not earthshaking compared to crime stories or nightclub fires, but it did signal a significant departure from the more traditional previous tableaux to a cabaret-style performance for the talented Vincent amateurs.

The article began by saying that practically all of Boston's first families usually found themselves, at this time of year, coping with one of their daughters in an overwrought state. "It's always around the time of rehearsals for the annual Vincent Show when female nerves reach a most exciting and arduous peak. Debutantes who can sing or dance well enough to be in the cast are inevitably worried about the innumerable dance steps and lyrics they must know by heart. Their slightly older sisters, who may have come off with flying colors in previous productions, never seem to be inured to apprehension as the feverish pace of rehearsals increases, due to the approaching time of the great moment itself when the curtain will finally roll up on another elaborate Vincent adventure."

"This year," the critic continued, "the Vincent has more at stake than ever with its cabaret show since it has an altogether new type of production. After a great many years of staging the usual sort of revue in the Wilbur Theater, it will now stage a sophisticated cabaret type of entertainment in John Hancock Hall, where patrons will sit at small tables and sip champagne. Naturally the singing will have to be better, the dancing livelier, the solos more clever, the pace swifter, in fact the whole thing will have to be smarter and quicker." No pressure there.

That morning newspaper described at length the build up and preparation for the great cabaret. Rehearsals were being held in the pink and gold ballroom at the Somerset Hotel on Commonwealth Avenue. An army of attractive girls bounced about inside in abbreviated shorts meant to engage an audience of husbands and suitors. Outside, passersby on Commonwealth Avenue could hear the sounds of high kicking dance routines and choruses warming up. Soloists were practicing both on and off key day and night until it seemed even the hotel walls screamed for mercy.

By 1936, prohibition had been repealed; the nation was slowly beginning to recover. A little libation could go a long way in dampening the criticism of amateurs trying to do their best to raise funds for charity.

That year Vincente Minnelli was directing his first Broadway musical, *The Show Is On* and the future legendary singer and arranger Kay Thompson was exercising her pipes on the nationally broadcast *Chesterfield Radio Program*. Closer to home, George Roberts and his Harvard teammates were leading the Crimson to a 15-1 record hockey season. In Boston, a no more important musical production was about to take place.

During rehearsal, in the Somerset ballroom four little brown wood nymphs (played by Miss Hope Blanchard, Miss Jean Tuckerman, Miss Marion Lawrence and Miss Betsy Jacques) frolicked about like "silvery-brown leaves falling into the wind" rehearsing their ballet-waltz number. At the piano in another corner of the ballroom Markie Byron and her cousin Margaret practiced their duet with soulful ardor, their clear young voices ringing true and on pitch. The song was classic Vincent show with a silly three note tune and lyrics that rhymed too often in the middle of a line.

I can imagine the dialogue that took place between these two young, single girls. "Oh, Margaret," Markie said to her cousin, "I do hope we can perform well. If we don't sound good, at least we can keep them distracted with our legs and these short skirts." My mother knew then what attracted men, in spite of the fact that she always acted completely blasé around them. At times later on, illness made her even provocative.

In another corner, a group of twelve women in Scottish kilts, high boots with tassels and drum-major hats were led by dance captain Miss Lucy Ducey. They were preparing for the signature drill, the dramatic finale for every Vincent show. The Vincent Drill, sixteen marching women performing precise and intricate steps, had its first performance in 1895 and became a hallmark of the shows. These "soldiers" were perfecting their drill routine, shoulder-to-shoulder, in sharp precision as they formed two lines folding into one down the middle of the stage. No one was allowed to smile. This was a serious endeavor.

Drifting about here and there were stately, lovely girls in picturesque costumes of silver with whole quantities of violets on their enormous poke bonnets.

"Let's get this over with so we can go see George and Elliot", Margaret impatiently said to her cousin Markie as they finished the last refrain of their duet.

"One more time, Margaret, I want to get this right. George's mother will be in the audience. She's tone deaf and will be all the more critical because she doesn't know the difference between a musical note and the sound of a drop of water." Markie was adamant about her future mother-in-law. But then, Markie was adamant about most everything.

The subject of Markie's future mother-in-law had not come up between Markie and Margaret since Markie was not yet engaged. George Roberts was still a sophomore at Harvard and George's mother, Grace, was keeping a careful but silent watch on the relationship. Markie could feel a shudder of disapproval each time they met. The silence between them could be felt by others.

"Okay, but let's finish by five and get going. The other dancers have been playing bridge all afternoon waiting for their turn to rehearse," Margaret noted, "so we'll be done and it will be okay for us to vamoose."

What Margaret really meant was that it was time to see THE BOYS, their Harvard sophomore football playing paramours. Their plan was to take the T to Milton Village and walk up the hill to Markie's house at 108 Canton Avenue. There they would be joined by George and Elliott fresh off the field from an afternoon football victory against another Ivy League opponent.

There was quite a predictable pattern to the meetings between the Byron girls and their male beaus. The custom of double dating then was a lot tamer compared to today. The couples would walk past the Milton Academy's front doors down Centre Street to the Milton Cemetery, where they would spend hours conducting a mild form of "engagement." Though Markie would say that early on George had crossed the line to indecent behavior, apparently he did not in the cemetery.

Although my mother and father came from the same background they were rarely on common ground. Dad was no student. Markie was brilliant and restless. As early as her teens the restlessness of mania was beginning its insidious intrusion.

Academy Headmaster Field wrote a summation of George's assets in the spring of his senior year in high school. "He has been captain of both the hockey and baseball teams and has played basketball, although basketball has figured little in his recent program. He has been president of the Athletic Association, and has just been elected Valedictorian of his class." *Conscientious, modest, unassuming…and endlessly reliable-words* of praise then that would become a portent for the future. Although Markie did not begin to date George until she was nineteen, she later proclaimed to me that when they first met on her front porch in Milton when she was fourteen, he instantly "raped" her.

After Markie came out in Manhattan she returned to Boston for the fall and winter debutante seasons of 1935. She joined the Junior League and the Vincent Club. In the spring she performed in the 1936 Vincent Show and began to do some modeling of hats for a local shop.

In 1934, Bonwit Teller of New York was sold to a man named Odlum although the name of the store did not change. Odlum's, wife Hortense, who had already been serving as a consultant, was named president of Bonwit Teller in 1938, making her the first female president of a major department store in the United States. The Odlums also retained a connection to the firm's founding family, naming Paul Bonwit's son Walter Bonwit as vice president and general manager. Markie got a part-time with the company, mostly as a hat and hand model. Later when Muffy had to go to work she followed in her daughter's footsteps, serving in the wedding department, where she assisted wealthy families with wedding dresses and accessories until her early eighties.

Along the way Markie fell in love twice, the first time was with the son of a neighbor in Milton, Nathaniel Clifford. She met "Nat" through her brother Ted when both Ted and Nat were assigned together as pilots in Italy in World War II. Her parents liked Nathaniel well enough, because they knew his parents were of good stock and respectable. When Nathaniel and Ted Byron were killed flying in Italy in the war, both families were devastated. Markie was completely distraught, and the incident may have intensified her later instability.

Her second love was a young Episcopal minister whom she adored even more than the departed Nathaniel Clifford. It is one thing to lose your paramour to a plane crash, but to have your parents say you cannot marry that boy, caused Markie great concern and agitation. Muffy felt that the young priest was a bad choice because, as a minister, he would be poor all his life. No one knows if Markie suffered a setback from this decision at this time. I did know that when George Roberts reappeared, she felt resigned to marrying him because she knew he would take care of her. Perhaps at first blush *endlessly reliable* seemed like an endlessly promising option.

In a 1970 letter to me while I was in college in Iowa, she wrote "I saw very little of George at any time prior to the winter I was nineteen and in the 1936 Vincent Show for the first time. About the third time in a row that I went out with him he grabbed me the way he did that first time on my front porch and suddenly raped me in his mother's car which he had borrowed for that purpose. Well, darling that was the beginning—and it produced this fantastic family. I was twenty-five when we married the first time, six years after dating your father off and on. I conceived you eight months after our first marriage."

"And you know what? It was all his idea that we should remarry after we divorced the first time when you were six years old and Teddy was just three. He kept calling me when you were in Texas, asking me to remarry right after I got back from Reno from the first divorce. He kept asking me to remarry him and simply would not take no for an answer—just the way he was about asking me to marry him the first time."

Then Markie turned to the usual litany to conclude the letter. "It is very important that you know that you and Teddy (George, Jr.) and Cameron are all the children of George French Roberts, Sr., your father. In fact, I had never even been made love to until he made love to me the winter after I came out in Boston."

"Well, that's enough for now, my precious angel baby. Don't let any man touch you. Just come home safely to me and bring your brothers with you. ALL MY LOVE, YOUR MOTHER."

The Young Marrieds

My parents' marriage ceremony was a sumptuous affair in the winter of 1943 just before my father shipped off to Southeast Asia in World War II as a second lieutenant in the U.S. Navy. For someone who neither believed in God, nor organized religion, Markie allowed herself to be united in marriage in a high and fashionable "godly" setting. The wedding took place at 4 p.m. on Sunday, March 13, at the Church of the Heavenly Rest in New York just across from Central Park.

The wedding was huge and grandiose, planned and executed by Muffy for her eldest daughter. Perhaps Markie chose not to object or maybe she really liked the fact that the church was and is located on Fifth Avenue directly across from the entrance to Central Park, a place she dearly loved to go.

"**Miss Lillian Mark Byron to Wed. Lt. George Roberts March 13,**" read the headline under Markie's clear eyed photo in the **New York Herald**. "Mr. and Mrs. Edward J. Byron of New York and Dublin, N.H., formerly of Milton, announce the engagement and approaching marriage of their daughter, Miss Lillian Mark Byron, to Lt. George French Roberts, USNR, son of Mrs. James Adams Roberts of Milton and the late Mr. Roberts. While her parents lived in Boston Miss Byron attended the Beaver Country Day School and later graduated from Miss Hall's School in 1935. She made her debut in the 1935-36 season at a dance given by her parents at the Ritz Carlton in Boston and was introduced at the Bachelor's Cotillion in Baltimore. She is a member of the Junior League and Vincent Club of Boston. Lt. Roberts was graduated from Milton Academy in 1934 and from Harvard College in 1938 and is a member of the A.D. Club, the Hasty Pudding-Institute 1770, D.K.E., the Harvard Varsity Club and the Harvard Club of New York. He is a grandson of Mrs. Robert J. Walker of Leicester, England."

It all read like the beginning of a perfect marriage. Only some things were not right from the very beginning. For one thing, Markie didn't seem to care for George's *endless reliability*. To her he seemed rather dull. Or

61

maybe it was his style. Unlike the Air Force pilot, Nat Clifford. When Nat's plane flew into a mountain in Italy in 1942, she said she married George to take care of her, but he wasn't taking care of her in the manner to which she was accustomed.

Following their wedding George was sent to Naval training in Champagne, Illinois. During the long hours of the day while George was at the nearby base, Markie knew no one there and was too much of a loner to speak to other service wives. To amuse herself, she began taking a nutrition course that set her on a path of lifelong food obsessions and undoubtedly contributed to the journey toward mental illness.

When I was twenty-five, married, and once again in college and studying in Iowa, I received a letter describing the course she had taken many years before. It is an example of the multiple preoccupations she developed.

"Diana darling,

In case you are a fixer of salads, I must tell you I took a nutrition course given by the Red Cross in Champagne, Illinois when George was stationed there in the Navy when we were first married—and they told us that lettuce is something no one should eat. It coats the lining of the stomach and prevents you from absorbing other foods. This is, of course, a very valuable piece of information, and I'm sure it's true, aren't you? They wouldn't have been teaching it in the course if it weren't. It was a very good course in general with lots of valuable information. I got the highest mark in the class on examinations. Incidentally, I started several sessions late.

Now you mustn't take housework too seriously. Men can make a slave out of you. One thing I have thought of is that while you are doing housework you ought to wear shoes with laces and no heels. Of course sneakers answer this description or some other shoe with no heel. That's very important. Wedgies won't do. But a platform is all right provided it's not a wedge. It has to be perfectly horizontal. You should wear this kind of shoe all the time.

I wish you would. If not the laces, at least the shoe without heels. Try to get them with some good support for the foot—to give the whole body support. You can have a slight heel taken off a good shoe.

Diana, darling, don't worry about anything I said in my last letter. You are happily married and you took care of all the details as you saw fit. You must not to worry about anything.

Well my darling, your Mummy loves you so terribly much. You will always be my little Baby to me. It's hard to believe that you are so grown up. I will say nighty, night and sign off here. All my love to you my precious Little Angel.

From your Mummy."
P.S. Write to me.

After Naval training in Illinois, Markie and George moved to Greenwich Village just before my father was shipped off to the South Pacific. I was born in August of 1944 while Dad was still overseas in the Far East. Dad and I did not meet until I was seventeen months old late in 1945. I don't remember the meeting, but was I told it was mutual love at first sight. I do know he came home in time for us all to move together into another apartment in Greenwich Village. My first memory of Markie is in the kitchen when I was two and Markie had just turned thirty.

Before she developed food fetishes and other phobias, Markie loved to make fancy dishes. One of her favorites was called bananas flambé. I watched Markie roll the bananas in confectioner's sugar, fry them in a little butter and drop them in some juice that made them light up in a puff of fire. I didn't want to eat them, but I wanted to make them just like my mother.

In the apartment, I remember sitting on the floor amid steel bowls of graduated sizes. Moss green wooden cupboards, the kind of unanimated color applied by a hurried landlord, loomed above my tiny round frame. I could just barely reach the knobs on the lower cabinets that held the steel bowls. I spread half a pound of confectioner's sugar across the linoleum floor between the cupboards. A few bananas were all I needed to reproduce Markie's favorite dessert. I peeled the bananas and rolled them enthusiastically into the powdered sugar. Although I would not ultimately get the chance to fry the bananas in the traditional butter and brandy, this activity was completely satisfying to a three year-old whose hands molded the silky powder around the bananas until I felt proudly satisfied in their completion.

Every wall of the apartment was green, the color of moss and army fatigues, in a somber mixture usually reserved for doctors' offices or other institutional places. The front door opened into a small foyer which led to a square living room covered in one huge red/brown Oriental rug. My parents' bed, which operated as a sofa by day, was right there in the living room just outside the kitchen.

At the time Markie was pregnant with my little brother, who would be called George Junior but would be nicknamed "Teddy" after Uncle Edward Byron. Like me, Teddy would be an August baby, though much more a child of a self-critical Virgo than his feisty Leo sister. In fact, all of us, including Markie and my grandmother Muffy, were born in August. Markie had already had one miscarriage following my arrival and had begun to show symptoms of increasing inconsistencies in her behavior in each postpartum period. Many days she would soak in the deep oval tub and talk to me while sliding the soap over her expanding tummy with broad slow gestures. She talked about bodies and warmth and the need to always be clean. I noticed that she shaved her eye brows, her arms and her legs with frequent regularity. In the tub she cupped the warm water with both hands and tossed it back around her neck in a neat little splash to be sure to clean her neck.

"Diana, you are so beautiful, like my sister Diana for whom you are named," she would say to me. "Not like the other one, Margaret, who was loud and noisy. But you are unlike my sister Diana who was frail and couldn't stand up to Muffy. Neither could I. Nor could my father. They all left in one way or another and I was left with Muffy. Teddy crashed in Italy. Don married an English woman and poor Dick became an alcoholic while living that silly hunting life in the horse country in Virginia. But you are here with me now forever, my precious baby angel. And you are strong and beautiful."

By then I think I already knew what frail meant. My mother was losing her grip too, retreating from me. *Why did she talk this way?*

"Why is she called Muffy?" I asked, not knowing how else to respond, as Markie swooshed handfuls of water up around her neck and over her back relaxing in the warm water. Then suddenly a quick a non-sequitur: "Did I ever tell you I was in four a cappella singing groups at Miss Hall's?" I did not know what a *"cappella"* was, but I knew not to listen too closely after that. It was too confusing.

Whether Markie was ever really in a singing group or not, I did inherit the music appreciation gene. Early on, music became a passion that has served me well and faithfully. In those days, vinyl records, or 78 RPMS, were all the rage. I was told my Uncle Charles helped to invent them or at least to invest in them. I liked to think that he was responsible for all the bright colored faces that appeared on the records and turned into streams of bold colors as the record spun round on the turntable. Louis Armstrong and his trumpet turned into gold and brown as he started to play and sing. There were always little free floating black musical notes that danced on the plastic platters next to the singer's face. I spent a lot of time watching music spin before my eyes while my father listened to Louis Armstrong.

Teddy's birth meant that he got his own room, complete with a makeover paint job in robin's egg blue to cover up the dull green that I hated so much. I was especially jealous of his arrival because it meant I had to sleep with my parents in the living room. Teddy's crib was white with wide cream colored slats that protected him from my curious poking fingers and nudging elbows. One day, when the front side was down, I turned Teddy over on his stomach no doubt to smother him in his sleep. I was never one to hide my jealousy or check my ego at the door. Teddy wore little sleeping gowns with a pull string at the bottom so that the gown would not rise up on him and perhaps suffocate him. Later he would have beautiful, blond curly hair and a disposition that meant he never complained. But right then and there I wanted to pull that string right around his neck to eliminate this new intruder who had come between me and my parents. Luckily, my father intercepted me on the way to making my final play with that string.

My father became a constant and affectionate caregiver, which was good experience for what was to come. He would sweep me up in his big athletic arms, toss me in the air and then catch me low down, my head just missing the floor and then squeeze me tight with love. I would squeal with joy and we would start all over again. He had a funny smells which I learned to recognize as Lucky Strikes, apple from for lunch and Bay Rum. He was all man-father to me and I wanted him all to myself. One day he tossed me so high that when I came down I was dizzy and threw up all over Teddy's brightly colored mattress pad. At the time, I thought, happily, what a pity that I ruined his little bed.

My father's every move exuded athleticism, physicality, and open affection. Even after I threw up on Teddy's bed, or when I spread the bananas around the kitchen or later, made designs on the walls with little Teddy's poopy diapers, Dad showed nothing but big warm love for me. My father gave me ample room to explore my somewhat odd creative urges. Each time I did something that made no sense, he gamely shot me nonsense question, "So, Diana, why is a mouse when it spins?" To my gaping open mouthed "huh," he replied: "The higher the fewer." By that he meant that something I did or said made no sense whatever but that it was okay with him.

After the war, my Dad worked for an insurance company. In his spare time he played semi-pro hockey with fellow alums from Harvard who lived in New York and guys whom he had played against from other Ivy colleges. He often took me to Rockefeller Center and spent hours teaching me to ice skate. He was proud of how quickly I learned. Afterward we would go to Howard Johnson's for cocoa. In our neighborhood in the Village, we would go on walks together and he would introduce me to people who passed by. I was introduced to the popular band leader Skitch Henderson and Gypsy Rose Lee, whose son would become my classmate at the Rudolph Steiner School. Dad was gregarious and outgoing, a man who met no strangers. I am happy to have inherited Dad's "friendly" gene.

One night, as I slept between my parents in the living room bed, I developed a winter fever and ear ache. Most little kids get a thermometer stuck in their behind to take their temperature. But my parents only had the oral kind. Four minutes after my father settled the mercury stick in under my tongue; I gagged and bit the glass tube in half. Slivers of silver mercury slid everywhere in the sheets waking Markie up. Soon large fingers filled my mouth searching for crystal chips, red dye and toxic mercury bits. I got a lot of pleasure watching my parents hop up and down to take care of me when all I had done was take a short bite out of a long stick. Later, I remembered that incident as the one moment in time when my parents were united, at least in their concern for their little girl.

An Early Education

W hen I turned three in 1947, my parents sent me to the Bank Street School in Greenwich Village, a trendy preschool for progressive parents, teachers and, so I was told, bright students. Precocious or not, the real reason I was sent there was because Markie was beginning to fade away after Teddy's birth. The school was a wonderfully nurturing place. What I loved best was that I got to have a whole easel to myself—both sides—and all the paint I wanted. Finger painting was just as satisfying as the bananas and powdered sugar, and I made sure I used up as much paint as possible whenever I could. Preschool was a lot more fun than home at the time.

In 1948 all four of us moved to 59 East 79th Street to a large second floor apartment with a fireplace in the living room and big windows in the two bedrooms facing the street. For security, the outside of each window was overlaid with thick black grillwork. My grandmother Muffy and my grandfather Edward already occupied a smaller apartment on the first floor. Whenever we went downstairs, we had to take our shoes off before entering their apartment. Muffy was a meticulous housekeeper.

Teddy and I shared the larger of the two bedrooms. Our bedroom faced the street, so it had a window with those metal bars on it. The room was a soft yellow with a linoleum floor made up of red and yellow squares with grey flecks embedded in each square. The room was large enough for Teddy's crib and my bed with lots of room in between for toys and a fat gray mouse that appeared nightly by the closet door. By now, Teddy and I were no longer enemies, but playmates, tiny comrades, often in each other's arms. Certainly the family pictures show me pushing him everywhere in his carriage, even after he could walk, which he learned to do very early.

A long hall stretched between the living room and the kitchen which was next to our bedroom. One day, while Ted was practicing his first walking steps, he called "Dinah, Dinah" and I came running down the hall to our bedroom. He was trying to cross the room unassisted on his wobbly legs. And he made it! But just as he got to the edge of the room to cross over the door sill, he faltered and grabbed the door next to the place where I was standing with my fingers carelessly perched near the hinges half way up the door. The door shut on my left baby finger and to this day that digit has no nail-a symbol of our childhood kinship. Later in the year he broke his nose chasing me down the hall in his nightgown. So we were even.

Ted and I had much simple and physical fun together in those days in the early 1950's. I was his teacher, his mentor, his pal and a pest all at once. In many ways we had no choice but to enjoy each other because the polio scare was everywhere and we could go nowhere. We weren't allowed to go out, not even to the park. We could only go up to the penthouse garden to look over the city and get what little fresh air we could until the city of New York and the country would be healthy again.

We were more than a handful for Markie who was becoming more fragile and exhausted by the antics of her two children. One day I realized I could crawl up onto the window sill of the big window in our bedroom. Conveniently, it had a chair in front of it. I crawled out into the space where the iron grill work jutted out from the window in the form of a kind of cradle, taking a pair of scissors with me. Suddenly, the window closed behind me and I was alone looking down on the street below. I could see there were a few people on the street but no one was looking up at me at this point I could see the green awning of our building from my second floor perch but the doorman on guard could not see me.

I wasn't really scared. I didn't think about the closed window. Slowly, I took the scissors out from behind me or rather from underneath me. I held a handful of my bangs away from my forehead and cut away. Handful by handful I cut until off all my bangs lay in clumps on the window sill and my forehead was fully exposed.

I looked down on the street next to the green awning that was the entrance to our building, 59 East 79th Street. People on the street were stopped in their tracks to look up at the little girl outside the window. People stared up at me until someone, some little boy, I bet, let fly with his pea shooter that landed a small pea bit in the corner of my eye. The doorman, Arnie, saw it all. Arnie rushed up stairs to our apartment. Later, much later, he told me in confidence, that my mother waited much too long to answer the door. She tried to make him leave but he insisted on entering, coming straight to our bedroom and saving the day. He opened the shut window and lifted me back in to safety.

The shorn bits of hair were presented to Markie while she was in the bathtub. To be honest, Markie was often absent while being present, vague while meaning to be helpful. She could be withdrawn from time to time. Later, much later, at her memorial service I would describe her as "childlike." But at the time what did a six year old really know about these things?

By Christmas, things were getting worse. For one thing I found the friendly bedroom mouse dead in front of the fireplace next to the Christmas tree. The mouse was pretty big and had broken a few thin little ornaments on the way to its demise. I wondered what was coming next.

One night I woke up to hear my parents arguing in the living room. "There is nothing here for you," Markie screamed clenching her fists and pounding her forehead over and over with the curled fingers of her right palm. "You are a criminal. You sleep with black women. You give them jewelry. I must accomplish this divorce right now on my own at all costs. You stole over $20,000 from your Harvard friends and have never given it back. I hate you, George. Take your goddam' regimental ties and go home to your mother!"

What was she thinking? This sweet man who walked his daughter to the Bank Street School every day? This man who swooped me up in the air, who put his socks over my shoes to keep my feet warm, who was teaching me to ice skate like a boy on the rink at Rockefeller Center and prevented the mercury from poisoning me? What was Markie thinking? Or was something terribly wrong? I didn't have much time to figure it out. Along with the mouse, my father was gone right before Christmas Eve.

Once my father was out of the picture, Markie seemed to thrive on the "accomplishment" of getting rid of him. She continued to say negative and evil things about him that I did not question. *Did I believe her? Absolutely.* A child will absorb outrageous and cruel things for the sake of keeping love alive with the other and only present parent. Markie never told us that our father had moved to Texas to work for the then budding military industrial complex.

Markie started dating. Teddy and I went with the flow. There was Nick, the lawyer with the dyed yellow hair and the German accent. Then there was the doctor who worked at Bellevue. Then the pale, insipid man named Elliott, with thin hair and a bow tie who had been my father's roommate at Harvard and a partner in those cemetery outings at Milton. And there were others in rapid succession who never came to the apartment and whom I never saw. Markie began staying up late, becoming sleepless and agitated and forgetting to eat, constantly bathing and shaving her eyebrows, legs and arms. Later I would learn from my aunts and uncles that my mother's illness caused her to throw herself at men without any thought of commitment.

Eye in the Wind

1950

For first grade I was enrolled in another "progressive" school, this one on the Upper East Side near our apartment. The Rudolph Steiner School is based on the Waldorf method. At the time I didn't really know what "Waldorf" meant, just that I was learning to knit and speak German instead of reading and writing. When my permanent teeth appeared, reading was introduced. I overheard one mother speaking to another parent outside Mr. Steiner's office referring to the learning experience at the school as a place where children "bury eggs in the sand" to experiment with hatching them. And then, in fact, I even tried it.

Now that the mouse was gone, Teddy and I shared our bedroom alone. Since we weren't experiencing much in the way of nurturing at the time I decided to try my own experiment in mothering. I placed a large brown egg between the cracks of my chubby little behind. I planned to keep it warm until morning when it would become a full blown chick. Instead I woke up to a cold wet orange blob stuck to my cheeks beneath me in the middle of the bed. No doubt I had squeezed my butt with a little too much expectation.

Then there was the business of chicken pox. By now it was already1950. I was six and Teddy had just turned three. It was the summer of the polio scare in New York City and elsewhere. We couldn't go to Central Park to play, we couldn't go outside, we couldn't go to the movies and we couldn't even go up to the penthouse roof. But we could get the chicken pox!

Teddy and I got it essentially at the same time. I was sick first with a lighter case. When it was Teddy's turn, the number of spots on his little body way outnumbered mine ten to one and he had a high fever. Toward the end, when we were both getting better, we slept in Markie's bed while she slept on the couch in the living room. Some days it seemed that we were all alone all day in her room. One night Markie fed us a plate of ham and ketchup in bed. Very soon we were both throwing up. We had eaten little for days and the combination of the fatty ham and the spicy condiment made our little bodies heave everything up. When Markie looked in on us she thought she saw her children's entrails on the white sheets. She was spooked senseless, but instead of screaming frantically she went into a catatonic state, mechanically closing the door and leaving us in a pool of catsup. In the middle of the night, I got up and pulled the sheets down from the closet and remade our beds while Markie slept on the couch.

To my little mind this and other incidents were disturbing. One day out of boredom I climbed on a kitchen chair near the table where Markie had placed a makeshift ironing board covered in an old sheet to cushion the top of the board. Markie was ironing a red wool scarf. Over and over. I put my hand up on the scarf to slow Markie's ironing motion so the scarf would not burn. The red wool of the scarf began to turn brown, the color of dried blood, from too many strokes of the iron. Just as I put my hand on the crimson cloth, Markie calmly did a neat stoke across my chubby fingers pressing down on my right hand as if it were a pancake about to be turned. Markie stared straight ahead at the wall in a catatonic state, her face affectless, while I cried out in pain. Suddenly, Markie snapped. She was back in reality. "Oh, my precious angel Baby, Diana, I love you so much. I am so sorry. Let's put a little margarine on that and the pain will go away". Whenever I look at my right hand even now, I see the faint scars on my ring and baby finger.

In the spring of 1951 Markie thought the polio scare for that year was mostly over. We no longer had to stay inside or worry about ever getting chicken pox again.

At school, Mr. Steiner began taking the children on field trips and to recess in Central Park. One morning, before I left for school, I covered my left eye with a thick mess of gauze and strategically placed strips of scotch tape. By then Markie wasn't noticing much and had begun talking to herself or to someone who was clearly not in the apartment. I could do almost anything I chose to do.

Before I left to get in the cab with the proxy (usually an older woman baby sitter hired to take care of children before they were called baby sitters) I made one last serious assessment of myself in the mirror that rested on top of Markie's dressing table. I sat on the peach satin cushion and gazed at my emergency bandage to see if I looked like a sweet little kindergarten Cyclops. Yes, genuine sympathy would soon be coming my way at school.

Recess came early on that day. There was going to be an outing because it was really warm. Afterwards the children would have lunch outdoors in Central Park. The New York Zoo, particularly the smelly bird house held little interest for me in light of my medical mission that day. The attention and looks I was going to get from my classmates were really what was keeping me going.

Or so I thought. Mr. Steiner lifted a bright yellow and red kite in the shape of a dragon into the sky high above us. I ran along chasing my classmate Billy Lee, Gypsy Rose Lee's son. Then I ran faster and faster until I was beside him and almost out of breath. I forgot about the eye patch and the importance of keeping my handicapped image alive. The patch started to flap in the wind and it was obvious I was running full throttle with two good eyes staring straight ahead into the eyes of Mr. Steiner.

Back in the classroom after lunch, Mr. Steiner asked me to come out from behind my desk. Everyone in the class was knitting with big wooden needles, knit one, and purl two, knit one, and purl two. He made me come up in front of his desk in the front of the classroom to stand in front of my classmates. "Diana, what made you wear that patch to school today to fool all of us into feeling very concerned for you?"

What was I supposed to say? That my mother was acting weird? That I hadn't heard from my father? *That my mother talks to invisible people and irons my hand?* I did not have an answer and for once stood silent in front of Billy and the others until I was told to go back to my seat to resume knitting. Fortunately, following the Central Park embarrassment, school would soon be over for the year.

It is interesting to note here that the Rudolph Steiner School, a product of German ideas of education and disciplinary training, chose to cross the Atlantic to freewheeling Upper East Side of New York. Heinrich Hoffman's satirical nursery tale, *Struwwelpeter*, first published in 1845, was supposed to inculcate in me and Billy Lee a proper sense of behavior by illustrating the dire consequences that await those who don't tow the line. *Struwwelpter*, "shaggy Peter," proved to be so slovenly with his unkempt hair and six inch fingernails that he was rendered unpopular with his classmates. Would this be my fate? No six inch fingernails for me: I chewed mine to the quick.

Deep in the Heart of Texas

I don't remember how we actually got to Texarkana in the summer of 1950. That's Texarkana, Texas, not Arkansas. We must have flown out there accompanied by our father, because I found a square silver carrying case the size of a large typewriter lying on my dad's bed shortly after we arrived. The case was covered in stickers that said "bon voyage" and had names of American cities plastered all over it. Inside the case were miniature liquor bottles of all different kinds: gin, bourbon, scotch, rye and vodka. Little jiggers were also there and packs of playing cards to entertain my dad who, as a single male parent in the 1950s, had had to move west with two kids he barely knew.

I don't remember my father ever talking about Markie, where she was or who she was with, while we were in Texarkana. And neither Teddy nor I ever asked. It was only later that we would learn from Markie herself about her stay at a state mental hospital in New York.

We lived in a temporary apartment complex on a military base built for all the white collar workers like our father, who were brought in from around the country to work at Day & Zimmerman, a military industrial company that was making munitions for the Korean War. After being cooped up in a submarine in the Far East during World War II and then in an office at the Dalton Insurance Company in New York, Dad found the change a respite from the stuffy society life on the East coast. Much later, I realized that moving to Texas for the duration of the Korean War allowed him to find relief from the stress of having a mentally ill wife.

The U.S. Army had placed the apartment complex just outside Texarkana proper, which, I am told, is a very proper town. Everywhere there was dust and dry wind. No grass grew in front of our apartment. Only dried mud. When it rained, which was not often, my feet sank heavily into the mud, sucking me down into the ooze so that I could barely put one foot in front of the other. And there were the frequent tornadoes, not big ones, but new and scary for me and Teddy newly arrived from the East Coast. And swarms of locusts came swirling by unexpectedly in the summer.

Not only do I not remember how we got to Texas, no one ever told us why we went there. My guess is, although I never knew for sure, that Markie freaked out one afternoon in the spring while I was at the Rudolph Steiner School. She was probably at home at 59 East 79th Street in the apartment above Muffy and probably started acting strangely. When Muffy came up to check on me and Teddy she found Markie in great distress and making no sense. She called George who by then, although he very much loved Markie, had obeyed orders to leave New York and had already taken the job in Texas along with his best friend Bill Moseley and his friend's family. With the consent of George and Muffy, Markie was admitted to a residential mental health facility. At that time custody in divorce was always awarded to the mother. George probably did not have legal custody of us but may have been awarded temporary guardianship while Markie was "away."

The first order of business for a newly single parent is to find reliable help. George Roberts found Vada. Vada was black, ample, and in her fifties, a grandmotherly sort who was constant and caring. She came every day before Teddy and I woke up and was there at night to tuck us in when Dad worked late or, as I suspected and did not hold against him, was out on a date. Vada could be just as brave as she was steady. One day a nasty copperhead snake made its way onto the mud square in front of the apartment. Before I even knew what it was, Vada took a broom and flicked the snake out into the road away from the plot in front of the apartment. She went straight inside to the phone. Suddenly an army guard drove up from the gatehouse at the entry of the complex, got out of the car and shot the snake on the spot. I was as impressed as I was scared.

Vada could be playful and adventurous, too. One day she appeared with her thick pomade and big rollers that "colored folks" used to straighten their hair. She let me play with them and "do" my hair. I had already grown my hair long since the time I cut my bangs in New York and could wrap my locks around the big curlers and let them be singed by the hot iron "process" that accompanies this hair ritual.

Vada had many talents. She could sing. She could play the piano by ear. She let me know that I could too if I wanted to. She told stories about her family and coming West to Texas from somewhere in Louisiana. She read *Mr. McBoing Boing's Roast Beef* and *Scuffy the Tug Boat* over and over until Teddy and I took turns reciting the whole story out loud. And she sang Baptist hymns and spirituals to us. Sometimes she sang slow and quiet, sometimes loud and fast with great gusto and rhythm and with hand gestures and stomping feet. I loved every minute of her entertainment. It wasn't until my dad took us to the movies in Texarkana for the first time that I learned just how brave Vada was in every way and how limited by circumstances.

The occasion was my seventh birthday. Teddy and I were with our father on the roof deck of a house in town at a party given by one of his colleagues at work. From our perch Teddy and I and the others could clearly see a tornado in the distance coming our way. We were already a little scared because we didn't really know what that cone like shape was bringing with it. After the cake and candles, the group decided to escape the storm until it passed and celebrate by taking Teddy and me to see the early show of "The Thing" at a movie theater nearby.

Once we got to the theater I became vaguely aware that there was more than one entrance and more than one booth from which to buy tickets. Just after we bought the tickets, as we were preparing to go into the theatre, I looked up and saw a whole long line of black folks proceeding up a long wooden outdoor staircase to a second story balcony entrance. In the middle of the row half way up the stairs was Vada holding on to the arms of her two young grandsons.

When the movie started I momentarily forgot about what I had just seen on the stairs. I was still slightly anxious about the image of the oncoming tornado and fairly distracted, but I soon realized the storm was nothing compared to "The Thing." Starting with the beginning credits, announcing James Arness as the creature from another world, I covered both of my eyes against the scary, monstrous being that dominated the screen for the next hour and a half. It wasn't until the movie was long over and I was safely at home in my own bed that I recalled the scene on the stairs outside the movie theater. I remembered how calm and resigned Vada looked standing on those outside stairs. This was the night I understood that she and her family were outsiders.

Until then I did not know that there could be even one moment of sadness or disappointment in Vada's life because she never, ever showed my brother and me anything but confident love. Every day she made me sing and want to play music when at times no doubt her heart must have been breaking.

Because of Vada, or maybe it was those old Louis Armstrong plastic records, I definitely wanted to make music. I wanted music lessons. I thought playing the piano would be the coolest thing ever, although the kids next door took lessons and hated them. I asked my father over and over when, could I please have piano lessons. He never really seemed interested, or maybe he thought I wasn't serious. We finally did get a piano and even though Vada could only play by ear, she helped me pick out tunes. She was right. I was able to do it! But I wanted to know all the parts so I could play and sing them together. In my small way I wanted to find a voice. But the lessons never came.

After the hot summer, by September 1951, it was time for me to go to school while Teddy stayed home with Vada. Every morning, a driver came in one of the military base's minibuses to take me to Saint John's Episcopal Day School fourteen miles away in farming country. Posted on the side of the road were signs for free manure and billboard ads for liquor stores and JESUS WANTS YOU! The driver of the bus never shaved or bathed, it seemed, and he chewed tobacco out of his left cheek. One day his wad went off the front window and into the back seat window where I was busy breathing fresh air and trying not to suffocate from the smell of the driver. The tobacco mess landed directly on my face, like some exploding rancid wet prune, and spread across my left cheek. When I told Vada and my father that night what happened, magically a new driver arrived the next day who did not smell, shaved daily and did not chew. He was a young military recruit assigned to "our detail."

Saint John's Episcopal Day School presented me with my first real reading experience. In New York, I had been busy knitting and learning French and German. Granted it was only first grade, but I began painfully pro-nounc-ing ev-er-y syl-lab-le slowly in the Dick and Jane books and was embarrassed that those around me were way ahead of me. I did not yet know I was a pretty quick learner for a kid who had been plucked out of the crazy Rudolph Steiner School in the heart of the Big Apple and dropped down in the middle of a cow pasture in Texas.

Recess at Saint John's was actually more interesting than recess in Central Park. For one thing it took place in the cow pasture where there were real cows right behind the first grade classroom. They had clearly invaded the school yard from time to time since there were hard dry cow flops everywhere that I and my classmates stumbled over or jumped on or tried to crush to bits with our sneakered feet. One day, I chose to sit on a large cow flop since it was piled so high and dry as to form a little seat.

Somehow I didn't see all those red ants making their way across the dried excrement and into the thin little panties under my smock. Soon the bell rang and I made my way back to the classroom itching and trying to extricate the ants without much success.

"Miss Diana, may I have your panties, please! Go behind the easel and put these on." Was she kidding? Asking me to change my clothes practically right in front of the class? Luckily the teacher had a pair of boys' trousers on hand for just such an occasion. I had the definite feeling I was not the first, and would not be the last, to experience, as they say, most often in a different context, "ants in my pants".

In 1951, my father was thirty-five and single. He had chosen to be a single parent. Even insanity was not a defensible argument against giving custody to the mother. Yet he knew Markie was not capable of being a mother. He probably didn't even have legal custody of us, but you had to give him credit. He was doing his best to raise two young children on his own in a state he knew little about. He couldn't really cook, but he frequently took his two children to the Buffet Palace where we filled our plates every night with the same things: turkey over stuffing and mashed potatoes with gravy, green beans and Jell-O with whipped cream. Dad had his cocktails both before and after we went to dinner. At the time I didn't know what cocktails were. I didn't care. Tipsy or sober, Dad was there for us. He laughed and smiled and sang to us off-key. Why shouldn't he date from time to time?

"The stars at night are big and bright (clap, clap, clap, clap) deep in the heart of Texas!"

One night Dad took Teddy and me to the movies after dinner at the Buffet Palace. It was eight o'clock, well past the 7:30 curfew our mother had maintained in New York as soon as the Lone Ranger was over. He told us to watch the movie and that he would pick us up after the late show was over. At the time, movie theaters offered two movies back to back for the price of one.

Our two movies ended at ten o'clock. We waited outside nervously under the marquee whose lights by now were turned off. Ten thirty came and went. Teddy and I were still standing on the curb outside the theater at 11:00 pm. I was scared because it was dark and the street was empty. Teddy was just sleepy. A half an hour later Dad came careening around the corner in the black Plymouth 1949 sedan, clearly concerned that he had missed getting back to us on time. After that Teddy and I got to see many movies and to stay up late "deep in the heart of Texas."

I always knew my father was dating but, as with Markie, I never met any of his dates. One of Dad's dates lasted an entire week-end. On Friday night Teddy and I were packed up and delivered to Vada's house for the weekend. We didn't know this, but on the Thursday before that weekend Vada's brother, Paul, named for Paul Robeson, passed away after a sudden, massive heart attack. The wake and the funeral were scheduled for the coming weekend with a huge church and community celebration of Paul's life.

In truth, I was looking forward to going to Vada's house to meet and spend time with her whole family. Why not? At this point Vada *was* family. She treated us with as much love as her grandsons. She was the mother who was there for me and Teddy. She was the father who was there for both of us. She was the housekeeper who was teaching me to pick up after myself, to brush my teeth and not to spill orange juice all over the kitchen table in the morning. She did the laundry singing through the washing and the drying on the lines outside the house. She taught me to make my own bed with "hospital corners" tucking the sheets under the corners of the bed to secure them from being dislodged by tossing and turning and kicking feet. She did this because my father's sheets were always a wreck in the morning after he tossed and turned all night.

I was really looking forward to seeing how things were done at Vada's house and by whom. I had met Vada's only daughter, Odine, who worked as a maid. It did not register on me that Vada and Odine were both maids, because my relationship with Vada was so much more like family.

According to Vada, Odine had two sons and two boyfriends. One son Odine had by her previous boyfriend. His best friend, now Odine's boyfriend, was the father of Odine's second son. Both guys engaged in petty crime and were serving time in the same cell in a prison in Kansas.

Odine's boys, nine and seven, were named Rosco and Antone. Vada called them "respectable boys with respectable names." Both were named after local black band leaders whom Odine also loved-literally. Vada loved those little boys with every fiber of her being, as if they were not just her grandsons, but her own children. She had the energy, heavy as she was on a five foot frame, to keep up with them along with Teddy and me.

Dad helped Vada pack our bags the week before so we could be ready to go when the school driver dropped us off at home on Friday afternoon. Dad never really said he was going on a date, but we knew.

Dad brought the Plymouth to a slow halt at the curb in front of Vada's house. My first thought was to wonder how so many people could fit in such a small gray box of a house. The box was essentially made of cinder blocks with a kind of patchwork tin roof. The cinderblocks had been washed chalk-white to make it look like there was a real finished outer layer, but the gray cement was peeking through all over.

As we got out of our car, Vada greeted us with open arms that wrapped around us in an octopus hug. A hug from Vada felt both incredibly tight and marvelously soft, like falling into a huge comforter or a down pillow where your body leaves its own imprint on impact. We were so loved we could hardly breathe.

Vada took our bag, which was Dad's s aluminum case with the bon voyage signs, and waved our father away with "Seeya Sunday eve-nin, Mistah Robbets."

Once inside the house, I saw that it was one large room with a big cast iron stove in the middle and little living places stationed efficiently around the big living space. There were two single beds that served as couches by day and were pulled together at night into a double bed where Teddy and I would sleep. A smaller room bordered on the living room where that night Vada and Odine and the two boys must have planned to sleep together to give us our comfortable berth. A homemade shower hugged the back of the house next to a small vegetable garden. The whole event was like a giant sleepover. In truth I thought this was a cool arrangement.

"My brotha passed yestiday, sudden, with a haat attack," Vada told us immediately. "We gonna celibate him with a wake and a suhvice this weekend. You kids will just have to atind and be paht the fambly". Vada never minced her words.

After supper we walked together to the funeral home, which was only blocks away. The funeral parlor was a mansion compared to Vada's cinderblock box. It was clean, clean, clean with white everywhere and smelled of strong doses of the same Clorox and bleach that Vada used a lot at our house.

The wake was in the main room of the funeral home. In the back of the room there were five or six empty caskets of varying sizes and quality with the prices on raised placards resting atop each one. The one nearest the casket in which Paul had been laid was empty and had a price tag on it marked: special sale, $85.00.

I felt intensely small but was able to look up into Paul's casket as we passed by to a seat down front. I saw the peaceful face of a very dark black man with white curly hair laid out straight in a clean white shirt, a black suit and the best spit-polished black wingtips I would ever see. I was sure that if only I were taller I would have been able to see his eyes looking back at me and a smile on his face.

After the wake we returned to the cinderblock house, where Vada helped me and Teddy get ready for the sofa bed. Vada made up the "sleep sofa" and I unrolled the neatly pressed white sheets and made the bed all over again to show Vada I could do "hostible corners" on this funny contraption. Teddy fell asleep immediately, but I lay awake until I could hear Odine snoring peacefully in the back room despite the night heat.

The next morning everyone rose to attend Paul's service-except there was no real service. The service processional was a walk behind the closed casket across a number of open fields dotted with cow flops. There spirituals and gospel songs that everyone knew except Teddy and me accompanied the walk. The mourners sang freely, passing the solo lines among themselves. I tried lamely to join in on some of the refrains. Behind the casket, the family entourage marched slowly en route to a grassy knoll strewn with wooden crosses and a few headstones of prominent and wealthy members of this black community.

On the walk to the gravesite and back, Teddy's hand clung to mine, and I was careful to take short steps like his so he would not fall behind me. He looked so out of place in his thin little khaki shorts, Buster Brown shoes and striped tee shirt amid all the grownups and the teenage girls with colorful print dresses. At five, he was too young for a crowd to taunt him as a little white sissy. I suspect they wouldn't have tried.

Back again at the one room house, the feasting began. There was a big open homemade barbecue pit outside between the shower and the vegetable garden, where pork and chicken parts of all sizes were roasting. Inside, there was the stove heated by wood, because there was no gas or electricity. Vada prepared all her food without a single measuring spoon. The measuring math was definitely in her head. I had already learned from her what a fourth of a tablespoon was, as well as how to measure a half a cup of any liquid or solid solely with my eyes alone. What a difference from Markie, who measured everything obsessively in the kitchen on East 79th Street: salt, ketchup, Campbell's soup, Franco American gravy, margarine, the kind with the red dot in the middle that you massaged so that it looked like butter, and perfume and cold creams and Jell-O and shaving cream. Not only were there no measuring spoons here, there were no cookbooks in sight. Actually, there were no books. Yet I knew Vada could read because she read to us daily. It was obvious Vada had learned to cook from her mother after her mother's hard day's work in someone else's home or standing on her feet outdoors all day in the field.

Being from Louisiana lent a special flavor to everything Vada cooked and touched. She sang to us and to herself frequently, but what she could do with a spoon as her instrument was amazing. She loved to prepare Texas crayfish with a Cajun twist. When it was time to test the "doneness" of the dish, there was a lot of stirring of her spoon, tapping on the pot in a kind of rhythmic pattern, sniffing of the stew and a general questioning of the readiness of the dish. She would add a pinch of something hot, then something sweet and then something sour until the whole thing came to a flavorful boil, the final movement, a symphony for the palate. She shouted phrases like "I be cookin' it until golden brown" or "you gotta treat it like mud!"

I loved every bit of that day, even though it was a time of mourning. How could anyone be sad when there were wonderful dishes I had never eaten or even heard of: crayfish jambalaya, dirty rice, Louisiana gumbo, barbecued everything, red beans and rice…..and marvelous spoon bread?

After the long day of grieving was over and everyone had gone home, many on the long trip back to Louisiana, I climbed on to the top of one of the sofa beds in the one room house just as the sun was setting in the early evening. I made sure Teddy was secure in his sheets on his side so he wouldn't fall out on the floor.

Odine, who was barely more than a teenager, climbed onto my side of the bed. She had a hot iron stick that she had been warming in the fire while the cooking was going on. She greased her hair all over with fancy pomade and then began wrapping clumps of her hair around the hot stick making her hair roll out straight with each effort. I loved watching her make the kinky little curls go flat. I asked her to try the exercise on me. I actually I hated having straight hair and thought the curling iron might help. Odine put the grease in my hair, then took one clump at a time and rolled my hair around the hot stick. Soon I had stiff greasy curls on either side of my face below my bangs. They did not bounce free and perky the way Shirley Temple's did when she danced with Buddy Epson in the "Good Ship Lollipop." They were new and fun and mine.

The sun was down by eight thirty, nature's way of turning lights out. I fell fast asleep, still full from the strange day and the fine feasting.

The weekend ended on Sunday afternoon when Dad came to pick us up. I was not looking forward to returning to the routine of orange juice, English muffins and Velveeta cheese back on the military base, but we were both glad to see Dad and ride home in the black Plymouth Sedan. Dad sang silly songs all the way the way home, one he said he had learned over the weekend from a friend: "When they begin the beguine........" Though I had no idea what the words meant, I was happy to hear him sing in his friendly off key way. Even if I wondered from time to time if Teddy and I were too much of a handful for Markie, I knew that we were more than a happy adventure for our dad. "Why is a mouse when it spins?"

One day in the summer of 1952, we were at the local country club. We must have been guests of a local member who was a golf partner of my Dad. At first sight I marveled at the huge inviting blue swimming pool with the baby pool built in at the lower end and the deep end with its lines and ropes for team swimming competition. Using my six year-old reasoning I thought I didn't actually need to learn to swim. It would just come naturally to me. So I jumped off the high diving board into the deep end. Very quickly I was choking, coughing, sputtering for air and treading water so hard on instinct that I was completely ineffective at staying afloat. Suddenly a very large laughing man was beside me pulling me by the chin out of the water over to the side of the pool where he handed me up to my dad who had just come in off the golf course. The very next day there appeared in the *Texarkana Times,* a photo of the man in a tall Western hat with me in his arms at the side of the pool. The caption read: SENATOR SAVES SIX YEAR OLD FROM CERTAIN POOL DEATH.

It seems I was always pushing limits, taking aim at every new target full tilt, practicing solo in the world. No one was really keeping check on me, and in some ways, despite the misfortunes, it was an adventure filled childhood. I did not know it then, but early on I was developing a resiliency, an inner strength and outward calm, to meet change and challenge head on wherever it might meet me.

Markie's visit came without warning because my father never mentioned it until breakfast the morning she was to arrive. It was Saturday, so Vada wasn't around and Dad was making French toast. I was soaking the slices of white bread in the egg and milk and Teddy was trying to pour orange juice into small glasses that had once been jars of jam.

"Your mother has come all the way out here and wants very much to see you for the weekend. I'll drive you in town to meet her." That was it, not where had she come from or where had she been.

We met in town rather than at the airport, at a hotel in the center of town next to the Buffet Palace. I was not yet wary of her and did not question why Teddy and I had not seen her in almost a year and a half. My dad did not explain her absence, or the fact that she didn't write and hadn't called. *Like she never left. Like it never happened.*

"My precious little baby angel, I have missed you so much! It's so wonderful to see you and be with you. You look so beautiful, baby. You are my own little baby girl. And Teddy, how sweet you are, my blond beautiful curly headed precious son, my little baby."

"Are you here to stay" I blurted out. Perhaps I was more wary than I realized.

"Of course I am, sweetie. I have lived my every moment for this day to come.

"And look at you, little Teddy. Look at those gorgeous blond curls. I just want to hug you to death".

Teddy moved toward me and put his little left hand in my left, the hand that had the missing fingernail. I could tell he was trying to hold his breath in preparation for whatever might come next.

Later I would realize Markie's visits were more like missions, and the mission was always the same: *get the children away from George who is a mean and cruel man who sleeps with black women and gives them diamonds.* Even though Markie was outwardly still beautiful, her mouth could say things that left this seven year-old dumfounded and disbelieving that such beauty could utter such foul things. I was too young to know what it meant for my father to sleep with a woman, so I was not worried about that, but I knew my father didn't give away diamonds he didn't have!

Dad was scheduled to pick us up on Sunday night following our sleepover with Markie after his golf game and dinner with his friend, the Senator, who had saved me in the deep end of the pool. I missed Vada during the weekend and was looking forward to seeing her on Monday morning.

Even before she arrived in Texarkana, Markie had already scheduled our flight out for late Saturday night so that my father would assume we were asleep with her at the hotel and that he could safely come get us the next day. Neither Teddy nor I knew where we were going or why we were flying in the dead of night. We were told we were going to live near our grandfather, Edward W. Byron, whom we did not remember well because he and Muffy separated soon after we were born. They divorced in 1950, when he moved back to Hagerstown, Maryland and married his second wife, Virginia.

We boarded the plane sometime around midnight. As we walked from the tarmac to the plane Teddy put his right hand in my left, pulling on my finger without the nail. I had become aware that this was his silent code for being scared and uncertain. I was scared too, but did not dare let my little brother know. Neither of us spoke. We wondered in silence why we never got to say good bye to our father.

In the Land of the Greek Gods

The Long Meadow Apartments were on the outskirts of Hagerstown and were very different from the military complex in Texarkana. For one thing there was grass everywhere in between the three story apartment buildings where there had been nothing but dust in Texarkana. The buildings themselves were red brick with white trim and white shutters around every window. There were lots of children on the paths where we might have ridden ride bikes if we had had them. We did not bring anything from our life in Texas except the clothes we were wearing that Saturday night.

The apartment was a third floor walk up: white and sunny with two bedrooms and a bath, a living room, dining space and a kitchen with a small panty. Although I was about to turn eight, I would soon start school in the second grade at the local public elementary school. Teddy turned five in August the week after me. He was still too young to enter kindergarten. There were no day care centers at this time, at least not in Hagerstown, and we couldn't afford a Vada, nor would Markie have wanted one. I was vaguely worried about Teddy spending all day every day alone with Markie.

At first we stayed with our grandfather while the apartment was being painted and readied for us. Grandfather Byron lived in the old Byron residence that had been occupied by his father during the heyday of the Byron Shoe Company. The house was made completely of lumps of round gray and white stone, and the insides of all the rooms were lined with dark stained wood. It is hot in Hagerstown in the summer and I was glad of the cool and the dark in this new, safe place. Grandpa was short and round and bearded and polite, with a slight lilt in his voice that was natural because he was essentially a southerner although he had spent much time in the North in New York and New England before divorcing Muffy and returning to his roots of the late '40s. He didn't seem to do much except read the paper and speak softly to his wife. I didn't understand what Markie meant when she said he was living off the "remains" of the Byron Company.

After several weeks, we moved into the apartment. One day, a half dozen huge barrels arrived. Markie said they were full of furniture and dishes and linens and coming out party dresses she had kept for years since her debut in Boston and New York. I wondered whom she was keeping them for. In fact, the only thing she ever wore were white tee shirts, navy blue shorts and some very strange looking green leather corrective shoes that she ordered from a catalogue after making me measure her feet with a ruler.

Not long after we moved to Hagerstown, her strange behavior began to re-appear.

"Why do we always have to have hamburgers and Franco American gravy with mashed potatoes?" Teddy asked, after a full week of this fare every night at 6 p.m. "And why do we have to take that horrible cod liver oil right after? It makes me sick."

I held my tongue because I knew there were bigger things to worry about, but I wondered why, during the few times I visited the apartments of other kids, they got to have canned corn, and LuSueur peas and creamed corn and Spam, things I was sure would taste better than brown gravy. At least we no longer had to push the red berry around in the yellow white goop to make it look like real butter. The war had been over for quite some time, but I could still remember the taste the lard that passed for butter.

The move to Maryland confirmed that Teddy and I were not living life like other children out riding their bikes in our neighborhood. I had already begun to feel separation from others my age and sensed this might last my whole life. The feeling of being different really began with the lack of a Christmas celebration that year.

Santa Claus was really never one of my heroes anyway, I told myself, not since my first memory of Christmas when Markie kicked my father out and told him to go home to his mother with his neckties. In Texarkana we had visited our neighbors, the Moseleys, and their tree became our tree when we shared Christmas dinner at their house. But it was not our tree, or our Christmas. At the Moseleys' house I learned to ride a two wheel bicycle. But it was not my bike.

To be fair, we had gone to the Christmas service at Saint John's, the parent church next to my school in Texarkana. That was where I first learned Christmas carols. I still sing "We three kings of Orientar" instead

of "Orient are" (to me Orientar is still a country next to Egypt) just to keep Christmas young and fresh as I was then. It was no surprise that my father's favorite hymn was "Onward Christian Soldiers." He wanted to be such a straight arrow, but he had been thrown a number of curves already in his young life. And now we had been taken from him again.

Then cameChristmas in Hagerstown. The tree went up but never came down. Two days before Saint Nick was supposed to come down the chimney we didn't have, Markie sent me to town to buy gifts for Teddy and me. I was nine years old and had never ridden a bus alone. The only bus I had ridden was the school bus with Teddy and our own personal driver. Why wasn't my mother coming with me? Did I do something wrong? Markie simply said she was not feeling well enough to come with me.

"Diana, go out the front door to the left. Turn right at the end of the sidewalk. Follow the sidewalk with the grass on your right until you come to the corner. The number 37 bus will take you in town and bring you back. Be my precious baby angel and bring back some puzzles for Teddy and the random House Book of Greek Myths for you and me." At times Markie could be forceful and specific.

"We will have such fun together learning about Zeus and Hera, whom the Greeks called Juno. You'll see."

January, February, March passed and still the bare branches of the Christmas tree stood in one corner of the living room with dead brown reminders of evergreen spilled over the floor beneath. A few round ornaments with faded chips hung on the fossilized branches above. The whole thing looked like a macabre piece of artwork created by some cynical modern sculptor who didn't care for the ritual of Christmas. The sculpture was real: an unplanned artful reminder of the Christmas that wasn't.

But we did read the myths. Actually the Greek gods were more fun to believe in than Saint Nicholas and a lot more plausible. I learned that these myths were a way of explaining natural disasters. This gave me the idea to invent a few myths of my own.

Markie made sure I knew all the key players on Olympus. Teddy was still too young to take them in. "Repeat after me," she intoned with the authority of one who really believed in these epic stories. "Zeus was known later as Jupiter by the Romans. He was chief. His two older brothers were the assistant chiefs. Though not as powerful as their younger brother,

Poseidon and Hades could claim equal status. For just as Zeus ruled the Sky, Poseidon was lord of the seas and Hades was the supreme authority in the dark underworld." Markie knew her stuff.

"Then there was Hera, or Juno, Zeus' wife. And Hera's son was named Hephaestus or Vulcan and his sister, Hestia (Vesta). Then there was Ares (Mars), god of war who was also their son. And Zeus's daughter, Athena." It was a litany well-suited to Markie's name calling and all the "begats" she often invoked from the back of her mind.

Markie told me over and over, in between the stories of these twelve Olympians, that she had chosen my name Diana, not in honor of her deceased sister after all, but so that I would be strong and beautiful like the immortal goddess. *Heady stuff for an eight year-old.* These twelve Olympians made up a divine family that we became a part of. Zeus became my Santa Claus and Hera, my heroine. I was the beautiful goddess of the hunt, Diana, known to the Romans as Artemis. The story of the Medusa, on the other hand, was not one of beauty but a tale of monstrosity which filled me with terror every time Markie began to relate it:

"In ancient Greece a gorgon was a terrifying female creature. Gorgon comes from the Greek word **gorgós**, which means "dreadful." I loved hearing Markie read the word derivations even if I didn't always understand them. She had a resonant soft, low voice that made all words sound interesting.

"The Medusa was one of the three Gorgon sisters. They were monsters who lived on an island and were known far and wide because of their deadly power. They had tusks like boars, protruding tongues, thick dragon scales, hands of brass, wings of gold, and faces so ugly that all who looked at them were turned to stone. Markie told the tale of Perseus slaying the Medusa, as if it were happening right then and there in our living room.

"Young Perseus was the son of Zeus and Danae. He was sent on a mission by an evil king to kill the Medusa, who would most certainly kill Perseus before he could kill her. The king wanted Perseus's Mother, Danae, to become his wife and did not wish Perseus to survive to return to protect his mother. Perseus boastfully promised to bring back the head of the Medusa as a wedding gift for the king and his mother.

On his trip two great gods watched over Perseus, Hermes, the guide and giver of good, and Athena. While Hermes directed him safely on his journey and gave him the sward with which to decapitate the Medusa. Athena gave Perseus her polished bronze shield. With caution she urged Perseus "to look into this when you attack the Gorgon. You will be able to see her in it as in a mirror and so avoid her deadly Power."

The Medusa was one of three sisters, called the Gorgons, but she was the only mortal one. Medusa was once so beautiful that Zeus's brother, Poseidon, had been crazy about her, but she didn't care about him so he turned her and her sisters into monsters with live snakes covering their heads. The Medusa kept her beautiful face but everything else was monstrous, and whoever dared to look into her face ended up being turned into stone.

"The location of the Gorgons was known only to the Gray Women, who were the sisters of the Gorgons. These women dwelt in a land where all was dim and shrouded in the twilight that the moon shone on that country. They were very old and withered, and had only one eye and one tooth between the three of them. They took turns with the eye: when one was done using it, she would remove it from her forehead and hand it to another."

"You mean they would just toss it around between them?" I wanted to know. Markie"s voice was low and sweet but without affect. She said nothing but read on. Teddy came in from his nap and cuddled beside me clutching his blanket. Still sleepy, he was not yet scared like me.

"Perseus, had a plan," Markie continued, no longer reading from a book, telling it freely from memory. "Because the Gray Women were the sisters of the Gorgons, he had to trick them. He kept hidden until he saw one of them remove the eye from her forehead. Then he rushed forward and grabbed the eye and refused to return it until they told him how to find the Nymphs of the North who would point him to Terrible Sisters' Island where the Gorgons lived.

Markie became highly animated just as the story picked up dramatic speed. "Luckily," she continued, "all three Gorgons were asleep when Perseus found them. In the mirror he could see them clearly, that they had great wings, and bodies covered with golden scales and hair a mass of twisted snakes. Athena now appeared beside him and told him which one was the Medusa. Perseus looked at them in the shield in the reflected light of his shield, and Athena guided his hand as he cut off her head.

"He decided not to antagonize the others and dropped her head into a pouch he had with him. He escaped southward and Hermes and Athena no longer guided him. Strong winds blew him across the sky like a raincloud, so he stopped to rest near the palace of the Titan Atlas, who refused him hospitality. As a punishment, Perseus showed the Gorgon's head to Atlas and turned him into a range of mountains that now bear his name."

Markie ended the story by telling us Perseus gave the head of Medusa to Athena, who bore it always upon the aegis, Zeus' shield, which she carried for him.

I loved the story mostly because of the storyteller, who was so totally alive and present when she was telling a tale, unlike other days with Markie. The image of the mortal Medusa with visions of slimy venomous snakes was firmly planted in my brain. No sugar plum fairies danced in my head.

The Arms of Medusa

1953

Sometime in April the old pink sofa, discarded by Muffy for something more current, arrived from New York and stood alone in the living room. Teddy and I sat on it at night huddled together in one corner listening on the radio to "The Lone Ranger" and "The Shadow" before lights out at 7:30 p.m. Markie said she planned to open the barrels, but she never got around to it. The brown cylinders were a daily reminder that we were not like other families. The salmon cover on the sofa was wearing out, and so were our spirits.

Markie had more than a few obsessions. According to her, our shoes had to be specially selected. We both had to wear Buster Brown oxfords with tight laces to keep our feet straight, straight, straight and our arches high. We were never allowed to wear sneakers like other children, whom we had to call "children" and never "kids." "Sneakers have no support for one's arches," Markie said, "and one must wear them with white socks always so that if you cut your foot you won't die of blood poisoning like F.D.R.'s son."

"Why can't we eat white bread and white sugar like other children?" Teddy asked. "And why do I have to sleep without a pillow anyway?" Teddy never complained after he asked the first time.

"White bread has sugar in it and sugar is pure poison. A pillow will give you a hump in your neck." When I asked if we could eat something besides canned meatballs and mashed potatoes with Franco American gravy, Markie assured me "all fresh foods have toxic chemicals in them." Only the best was good enough for her precious Angel Babies.

I kept things inside myself and wondered silently: was Markie strange or just tired? Why does she want me to call her Markie when other children say "Mommy?" I missed Vada a lot, especially at mealtimes.

Then there were the bath talks, the same old ones about shaving and cleanliness, but Markie never talked about the one really big, obvious question that was forming in my head. Was Markie pregnant? She had told us sometime earlier that she had remarried my father, George Roberts. But why wasn't he here? Didn't he want to be with us? Why hadn't he come to get us before now?

I didn't know how long a pregnancy was supposed to last, but Markie looked pretty round. She looked the way she did before Teddy was born. She never mentioned that she must have been visited by our father sometime around Thanksgiving the year before. Or met him that weekend in November when we stayed with our grandfather and Virginia and Markie went to New York, she told us, to visit her mother. We still only talked about the need to shave my eyebrows and arms when I would grow up and that I must strive always to be completely clean and hairless.

"Don't be scared, sweetie. Being clean is being healthy and I want the best for you, my precious little baby angel." She never mentioned that I soon would have another sibling. More than a year had passed since we moved to Maryland. Instead, she talked about what it would be like when I would become a woman. At nine I was fully informed about the advantages of Tampax over Kotex. Later, much later she would counsel me via letter on how to take the inners out of each Kotex before using it. She would send strict instructions on avoiding lettuce and sugar at all times. Was she ahead of her times or just plain crazy?

In late summer of 1953, Teddy and I were sent to stay with our grandfather and Virginia while Markie was in the hospital. Ten days later Markie arrived at our grandfather's house in a cab. She brought with her a baby boy born on August 21, the day before my birthday. She had named him Cameron. Markie said he looked like his father. He was sweet and brown eyed, with a full head of dark brown hair, beautiful and healthy. I was glad his birthday was right before mine, Markie's the day after mine and Teddy's a week later. In my nine-year old mind I thought now we were going to be a close knit since we were all born in August. Maybe everything was going to go smoothly from here on out. The Christmas tree would go away, Markie would open the barrels, and a wonderful, fully furnished living room would appear! I could even invite neighborhood children over to my house to play and have a real birthday party with balloons and "Pin the Tail on the Donkey."

Only it didn't quite work out that way. There were no birthday parties that August.

We moved back to the apartment at Long Meadow with Markie and our new little brother. The barrels were still there when we opened the door and the brown prickles from the tree were still spread out on the floor at the base of the tree which was by now just a skinny, dry stick.

The first thing Markie did was bathe Cameron in the kitchen sink in warm water. Then she made a makeshift bassinet by lining the top drawer of her bureau with two pillows. She placed Cameron carefully on the pillows and tucked him in safely with a blanket. Very smart, I thought at the time. I remembered Teddy's crib that time when I wanted to eliminate him, and I thought this was a much safer way to protect a child from anxious siblings. But by now I was no longer the jealous older sister and had become a partner with my younger brother in the act of survival. I had no idea I would soon become a "little mother."

Markie never talked about our father. He did not write, or if he did Markie hid the letters, and we did not write to him, but we thought of him often and missed him very much, though we were afraid to say so. Once when we inquired about him, we got back the all too familiar Markie monologue: "That murderer, he gives women jewels to sleep with them and they are black and he never was able to take care of me. He is evil. You do not ever want to see him again."

But we did want to see him, hear from him, hear him singing off-key and laughing.

One day we got our wish. I heard Markie on the phone with him. "Yes, he is healthy," she barked sounding irritated. "He weighed eight and half pounds. I am glad you like the name, but I really must get off the phone now."

I grabbed the phone from Markie's hand before she could replace it on the receiver. "Hi, Daddy, how are you?"

"Just fine, Miss Sunshine, but I miss your sweet smile. I miss all of you, I mean you and Teddy and now Cameron whom I have yet to see."

His voice sounded so familiar to me that it made my throat ache. Before he could finish another sentence, I burst into tears and began to cry uncontrollably. Teddy came over to put his arm around me and to try to get in on the conversation with Dad. Markie beat Teddy to the phone and took it away from me.

"That's it, George, that's enough. Thank you for calling." Markie didn't exactly slam the receiver down on the phone, but the connection was audibly broken that instant.

In the fall of 1953 I entered the third grade in the Hagerstown Elementary School. I was supposed to be in fourth, but I was still a little behind because of the knitting at the Rudolph Steiner School and the jump from Texarkana to a new school in Hagerstown. Late in the fall just before Thanksgiving, I was told to go home over vacation to learn on my own Roman numerals and the Palmer method of writing in a book on my own in order to jump into to the 4th grade several weeks after Christmas break. I spent many hours getting ready to write from I to CCC and to script the alphabet in a proscribed but not very beautiful hand. I was smart enough to do it even without Markie's help. I learned the Palmer Method on my own. .

Teddy, on the other hand, was not going to be allowed even to go to school to start first grade. It all had to do with Dr. Jonas Salk and the advent of the polio vaccine. Even though the actual vaccine would not be approved for use until 1955, Dr. Salk already had Markie's "no" vote when it came to her son. On the other hand, it was okay for me, the strong one, to have a shot in the arm at school.

The polio epidemic was considered the most frightening public health problem of the post-war in the United States. Annual epidemics were increasingly devastating. The 1952 epidemic was the worst outbreak in the nation's history. Of nearly 58,000 cases reported that year, 3,145 people died and 21,269 were left with mild to disabling paralysis. Most of the victims were children. Citizens of urban areas "were terrified every summer when this frightful visitor returned," according to national news reports. Apart from the atomic bomb, America's greatest fear was polio. As a result, scientists were in a frantic race to find a way to prevent or cure the disease. President Roosevelt, the most recognized victim of the disease, founded the organization that would fund the development of the vaccine. Since Markie firmly believed Roosevelt was a Jew like Salk, she was bolstered in her double opposition to sending Teddy to school where he would surely be inoculated one day. But it seemed okay for me to go.

"No Jew is going to inoculate my son," Markie repeated whenever I said I wanted Teddy to come to school with me. "Why is it okay for me to go and not Teddy?" Always one to harp on fairness, I continued to press. "Either I stay home with Teddy, or he comes with me." Reason was not on my side and Markie was adamant about the Jews being crazy people who wanted to kill her son with a vaccine.

And what about her other son? One day when I came home after school, I noticed Markie's daily uniform of blue shorts and tee shirt was all rumpled. She had spilled something that looked like apple juice all down the front of her white tee shirt. I smelled something very strong and unfamiliar when I got close. She was smoking a cigarette from a pack marked Pall Malls. She never smoked. There were many more in the makeshift ash tray made from an empty Franco American gravy can.

I had never before seen Markie take a drink, only my Dad. Markie smelled so strong it was hard to breathe near her. Dad did not smell like that. He drank anything that poured but he did not reek. I wondered how long Markie had been drinking and smoking that day to make her smell like that.

That evening marked the end of the first day of the complete transformation of Markie's personality from mother to monster. She became the Medusa. Her hair was disheveled and hung in wild clumps that jutted out from her scalp like the snakes on Medusa's head I had seen in the Random House Book of Greek Myths. She looked like the drawing in the story of Perseus slaying the Medusa. After Perseus chopped off her head with his sword, the snakes squirmed and slithered while he triumphantly held up the severed head before dropping it in his pouch. At that moment I wanted Perseus to chop off my mother's head.

Markie sat on the couch in front of the unpacked brown barrels drinking long into the night while gazing at the Random House book of Greek Myths. She was reading them out loud. Markie intoned in a flat, affectless, sing-song voice. Sometimes she read the same story two or three times. After each story she talked to herself about George, the Evildoer, his brother Jim, Man of the Underworld, George's mother, Grace Roberts, the Grand Matriarch, and her two daughters Martha and Grace, the Vestal Virgins. All were trying to take Markie's children from her. She would never let them. She would call on all her forces. She must stop them, protect her children from them. If she couldn't she might have to take drastic steps to keep her children with her wherever that might be.

Just before the Lone Ranger was over and when Teddy and I were going to go to bed, I looked in on little Cameron. He was sleeping in his drawer, but soon after we got to sleep, he woke us up howling hungrily into the night. He was competing with a catatonic mother babbling about her interfering relatives. I got out of bed several times in the night to give Cameron sips of water from an empty coffee cup. I had no idea when he had last been fed since I had been in school all day. I woke Teddy because I didn't want to be alone, but he did not know what to do, either. Cameron must have been very hungry but the water soothed him back to sleep each time. I put him in bed next to me and held him close.

The next morning Markie seemed to be okay until she announced "I am going to invite the neighborhood children to join us here while I read to all of them and you today. They will love the Greek myths as much as you and do I am sure." The hitch was she was naked.

"What about feeding Cameron? He needs milk or something. I don't know. You can't let him cry like that."

"He's not really my child. George raped me while we were not married, because he wanted to keep me. Let Cameron be. He is not part of us."

"We must feed Cameron first. No, Markie, please, no children here. I can take the book to school and share it with them," I quickly offered as an alternative.

"By the time I was your age, I had read all the great myths in Greek and Roman mythology. And I read them in French because we were living on the South Coast of France in Le Toque. Muffy made us read them every day. We must educate our neighbors' children."

Markie talked endlessly and repeatedly about her growing up days. About Poseidon and Medusa and George and how Athena interfered. I feared she might subject the neighborhood children to her litany.

While she rambled, I went to the bureau and carefully lifted Cameron out of the top drawer. He was fully wrapped in a soft white blanket except for his tiny red face and was screaming so hard you could see his tummy muscles moving. I could feel his wet diaper needed to be changed, but thought first I should get him some milk or at least water. I held him close as I moved to the icebox in the kitchen and he yelled and kicked. With

one free hand I made a bottle of water for him and put it in one of the baby bottles sitting empty at the edge of the sink. Then I realized that in order to warm up some milk, I would need to first put Cameron back in his drawer for a short period of time. Fortunately, he stopped crying while sucking on the water bottle. I was able to put him down and returned to the kitchen to warm the milk. When I returned to the bureau with the warmed milk, Cameron had stopped crying, somewhat sated by the water.

I lifted Cameron out of his makeshift bed, changed his diaper, rewrapped him in his blanket and sat down on Markie's bed to give him his bottle. I rocked him gently while he sucked the warm milk. Pretty soon, without finishing the bottle, he fell asleep with what I thought was a smile on his little face.

At the same time while Markie was on the couch, there was a knock at the door. This was strange, because no one ever came to our apartment since Markie had no friends and mine were only at school. I had put Cameron back in his bureau and moved quickly to open the door just wide enough to the point where the bolt on the chain allowed an opening of about three inches.

"Are you and your brother okay in there?" Dr. Butterfield asked. He and his wife and three boys lived just below us on the second floor.

"Two brothers," I corrected him. Yes, we are just fine, thank you," I quickly shut the door. *Doesn't every kid in the face of shame and embarrassment pull back, close the door?*

Was it shock or shame that made me close the door? At first I was startled. Then I wanted to appear to the doctor that everything was okay, that there was nothing weird going on in our apartment. I may have been too young to understand the concept of shame associated with protecting an abusive or ill parent from the reality at hand. There was no way I could bring myself to call the police or any other possible protector nearby like my grandfather. I did not know how to reach my father. And I wouldn't have tried if I did.

Hearing the conversation, Markie stood up and walked stiffly into the bathroom. The bathroom had always been our meeting place. Whenever she took a bath, I would sit on the toilet, seat down, and watch Markie shave her legs and arms and just talk to her about my day, my school, and the children in my class whom I could never bring home. Then Markie would begin the mantra about her life growing up. "I came first, older by two years than my next brother Ted who died in the war, then Margaret who had nine children, Don who married the English woman, next Dickie the drunk, and finally Diana, who died because Muffy killed her."

Over and over again she talked about Dad: the murdering man who dated black women and gave them diamonds. By now I could count on the litany and knew it by heart. These meetings were odd but comforting in a way that was predictable. It was pretty much the same as our life in New York had been after my father left. When Teddy was born, Markie became strange and now that Cameron was here, the routine was becoming déjà vu.

Only this day when I followed Markie into the bathroom to join her in our ritual, Markie suddenly pushed the white door shut just as I was about to enter. At first I thought Markie just wanted to be by herself for a little while. No big deal. Then I was worried she might hurt herself in there because she might still be drunk from that brown stuff the night before and unsteady on her feet. I started to push against the door gently to open it. Then I realized she was pushing twice as hard on the other side against me to keep me out. Markie began mumbling a mantra: "I can't do this anymore, I can't do this anymore, I can't……" I could hear the water running in the sink on the other side of the toilet which was just inside the door on the right. Did she want to take her bath alone, to shave by herself this time without me there? Did she want to escape me … or hurt me?

Suddenly Markie let go, the door blasted wide open, and because I had been pushing with all my nine year old might, I fell into Markie's open arms. It was not the hug that I expected. It was not a hug.

It was the Medusa, all arms and snaky hair clumps wrapping around me, suffocating me. Markie held me in her grasp, forcing me down, down, on my knees in front of the toilet bowl where the lid was up. I could not turn my head to look up. Must not turn my head to look up. If I did, the Medusa would turn me into stone. The Medusa *was turning me into stone.*

Markie shoved my head down into the urine-colored water. As I went down I glimpsed the word "Kohler" on the back side of the bowl. Markie's eyes were glazed and vacant, but her strength was savage, ten times stronger than normal. Her gaze was on fire. Was I doomed? Why was I put in this foul water? Were the Gods or Markie punishing me?

She pushed my head further into the white bowl where the water flushed down and out. I sputtered, coughing hard, choking on the urine rushing down my throat. I couldn't breathe. I couldn't scream. The yellow water filled my nostrils, hurt my eyes as my lashes filled with the stinging liquid. I gulped the urine in the bowl trying to get some air into my lungs. Trying to suck air out in spite of the liquid made me choke harder, spitting up the yellow water. Markie's hands grew even stronger now, keeping me from getting up and out of the bowl. My head was in the water for what seemed a really long time although it was only seconds at most. Finally, she released her right shaven arm from my head pulling my hair back until I was forced to stand up. With the other she flushed the handle up on the left. I swung free from the Medusa's grip still coughing, choking, confused. Terrified, I bolted from the bathroom doorway into the hall looking for my brother.

Suddenly Markie cried out, herself terrified, "I am so sorry, my precious little Baby Angel, you are my beautiful first born whom I love with all my soul. What have I done? Oh, sweetie, let me dry you off and wash your mouth of that horrid toilet water. I can't believe I have done this." *Neither can I. Is that all?*

I didn't know it then, but the incident would become an ever haunting memory of shame that would hold me back painfully at times in relationships and actions, like a virtual and invisible albatross around my neck lingering and growing larger as time went on.

One day not long after I came home from school still afraid of what I might find,

I saw an ambulance parked at the edge of our unit, not out back where no one would see, but out front to one side in broad daylight. I bounded up the stairs to the third floor, passing the Butterfields' apartment. Descending the third floor landing were two guys pushing Markie in a wheelchair, down the steps one step at a time. Markie was sitting in the wheelchair held motionless by a white canvass jacket with sleeves that had been crisscrossed over her chest and tied to the chair on either side so that she could not move them to hurt herself or anyone else. I raced up the stairs past the men, trying not to take in what I had just seen, in search of my brothers inside apartment 3A.

I need not have worried. Inside the front door were not only Teddy and Cameron but safety and salvation. Dr. Butterfield knew to call him. I burst into tears as I ran into the waiting arms of my father.

"The stars at night are big and bright (the anticipated clap, clap, clap, clap) deep in the heart of Texas," he sang softly in the familiar off-key. Teddy was already on Dad's lap. I pushed my way in between his legs to find a space so we could each have a piece of him. Teddy and I had not seen Dad for a year and a half. Our father had never seen Cameron. He was the same gentle soul with the big grin and the big hands and the hail-fellow-well-met smile. He could not kill a flea or murder a grown woman. I knew he would never be away from us again except in death.

Dad was quite the optimist. Either that or he loved Markie so much that he wanted to make things work at all costs. Dad stayed with us in the apartment while Markie was what we each referred to as "away." As the weeks passed, Dad talked about renting a house in Hagerstown so I could stay in the same school and Teddy could at last follow in my footsteps. He would see if he could get a job in an insurance agency, maybe the Hartford, where he had previously worked in the New York office. Maybe they would find a place for him in the Baltimore branch. A woman whose name I never knew came in daily to take care of Cameron. While I was at school, I knew Cameron was safe. Things were all going to work out when Markie came home. Dad was sure of it.

Markie did come home about six weeks after her stay at a local residential treatment center for the mentally ill. Dad had found a house to rent near my school. We had nightly meals together at the end of the day, when Dad came home from looking for a job. He broke the hamburger and Franco American gravy cycle and for the first time we had chicken pot pies and Jell-O with fruit inside and salad. Dad introduced variety that we had long been missing in our diet since our days with Vada. Markie often sat quietly in a chair at the dinner table or on the sofa too big for the small living room we shared.

At night Dad would read to us. Not the Greek myths but much lighter, fun literature for children. He introduced us to *The Wind in the Willows* and *The Tale of Peter Rabbit*. Now that I could read well, he wanted to hear me read to Teddy. I got hooked on *Little House on the Prairie* and would read to Teddy about the family that moved from Wisconsin to the prairie and became friends with the Indians. I wanted to be the writer, Laura Ingalls Wilder.

Often at night we asked about Vada. Did she miss us? Where did she go? What happened to Odine and the two boyfriends? Dad said that Vada was heartbroken when we left. When Odine said she wanted to get away from ever having to deal with the men in her life, Vada took the opportunity to move from Texarkana back to Louisiana where she got a job in a hospital in New Orleans. She told Dad she lost her brother and her two "lit luns", Diana and Teddy, seemingly all at once. She did not want to work for another family. She just wanted to tend to her daughter and her two grandsons in the future.

I was sad to know I would never again see my Vada, yet glad to know she found a new life. I did not realize at the time we too were headed for a big change.

One day I came home on the bus to the new house we were renting. The house was on a corner where the bus could easily stop to let me off. As the door of the bus swung open and I stepped down onto the curb, I witnessed a repeat of a previous scene in front of me, my classmates and others on the bus.

The wheelchair was being carefully moved by two big guys down the front steps of the house. Markie sat motionless in the chair, her arms once again crossed held to her sides by cloth strips tied to her hands and tied to the sides of the wheelchair. Her hair was disheveled. Some kind of white powder covered her face and so much deep red lipstick was smeared around her mouth that she almost resembled an immobilized circus clown. I was not surprised, only embarrassed.

It was apparent Markie would be gone again for quite a while. Dad moved quickly to tell us we would be leaving Maryland for Philadelphia to visit the family of his friend, Bill Moseley, who like him was finally returning to civilian life from Texas. Cameron would be left to stay behind with his grandfather and his wife, Virginia, who had come to the house daily to care for him until Markie could come home. Dad did not have legal custody of us and was taking a risk to remove us from our mother. I didn't know what my grandfather thought of this arrangement or his general opinion of my father given all the accusations Markie had made about her evil husband. For a long, long I would wonder just when Markie and my father got together, resulting in my little brother since we never saw Dad until Markie fell apart after Cameron was born.

With Markie again hospitalized after Cameron's birth, my father was faced with some major decisions. Should he stay in Hagerstown and settle there waiting for Markie to recover? Whom could he turn to for help with this? He decided on Bill Moseley, whose family had been our neighbors in Texarkana. The Moseleys had returned to Pennsylvania and were settled there. In early February, 1954, we were welcomed to stay, for the next several months, with the Moseley family in Chestnut Hill, just outside of Philadelphia. By summer we would be back in my father's home town in the house he grew up in outside Boston, in Milton, Massachusetts.

As we were leaving Hagerstown, I was certain of only one thing. I did not want to see my mother again for as long as possible. I welcomed the good bye. I would be sixteen before we met the next time.

On Centre

Summer 1954

U p until now I had been the target of just plain bad life circumstances. The toilet bowl incident in Hagerstown was just one in a series of childhood mishaps. But now there would be much to mitigate the feeling of shame I had long felt about being an outsider.

I was curled up in a wicker chair on my grandmother's sun porch in the summer of 1953 in Milton, Massachusetts, reading a Signet Edition biography about Dolly Madison. I was at ease for the first time I could remember since Markie's commitment in February.

I was going to be ten in August and Teddy would be seven. We had arrived in Milton just three months before the end of my fourth grade year and were beginning to take aim at the world. This was a new day, a spotless life, a perfect time. I was going to make the most of this on my own terms.

Now I had aunts and uncles who came to see their mother, granny Roberts, frequently. I welcomed being part of a really large close knit family. All six of Granny's children lived nearby in Milton and we spent lots of time together. Aunt Martha was the oldest. It was said that after graduating from Milton Academy she spent one day at Smith College before coming home for good. She later married a man from Fall River named Eugene Sullivan who was Catholic, a foot shorter than Martha and a brilliant doctor who became head of the Veteran's Hospital in Boston. From time to time Uncle Gene served as the family physician to save the cost of going to doctors during emergencies. Aunt Martha and Uncle Gene had three children who were my first cousins: Roger whom we called "Joe," Rachel, who was two years younger than I, and Martha, who was called "Boo" because she was a late-in-the-marriage surprise.

Next there was Grace, called Sis, who married Charles Clifford, brother of Nat with whom my mother had been in love before both brothers died in that plane crash in World War II.

Dad was next in line. Born in 1916, he suffered from rickets as a child and had to be nursed back to health by his mother. Perhaps because of early need for extra care, he became, according to many, Grace Roberts' favorite child. After his illness George was given piano lessons because it was thought his legs might never grow strong enough to play sports, but in elementary school he began to show real prowess in athletics.

Granny Roberts attended all of George's athletic competitions in school and later at Harvard. Aunt Sis, in a moment of indiscretion, once told me that on the day of the 1938 Harvard/Yale football game Granny took out a full-page ad in the ***Boston Herald*** publicly cheering the team on to win. In private, before the game, she urged her son not to marry Mark Byron, because she knew Markie was not stable and had already been institutionalized, perhaps more than once. Harvard won the game 7-0 on the field at Yale in New Haven and Dad, probably overjoyed, paid no attention to his mother's warning.

Edward Pierce Roberts was next to last, two years younger than George and not much of an athlete or a student. The baby of the family was Charlie who died young of cancer.

My cousins were close in age to me, and I enjoyed getting to know them, playing sports with them and spending holidays together. Often, when I came home from Milton Academy with cousin Edie, who was a year older than I, we had a special ritual. On the floor in every room there was a register that blew hot air into the room from below. Edie and I would take turns washing our hair and then drying it lying down with our hair spread out over the register- all this while watching Dick Clark on American Bandstand in Philadelphia.

One day, all too soon, Dad told me that Markie had been released from a mental hospital in Maryland. She was coming to Boston and wanted to see all three of her children together. She had picked up Cameron from the woman who had been taking care of him in Hagerstown and would bring him with her. She had been released from the mental hospital just days before and wanted to visit us.

My decision was instant, intuitive and made out of sheer self-protection. I wasn't thinking about seeing my little brother Cameron or advising Teddy not to go see Markie. It was the toilet bowl or the dried up Christmas tree or the albatross, call it what you will, that rendered me immobile when I thought of having to see Markie again. I could not make myself go to her. I was too young to recognize sheer survival instinct in me that I would call upon many times in the future.

I remained firm in my refusal. She would not be coming to the house. She was going to stay at the Essex Hotel. I refused to go with Teddy to see Markie, because I feared she would persuade me to go somewhere with her the way she did when we left Texas for Maryland. Teddy never refused anything and went dutifully to see her. Dad deposited Teddy at the hotel to spend time with his mother and Cameron, six years his junior. At seven, Teddy had still never attended school. By the next morning both of my brothers were gone. It was like Texarkana all over again. I didn't learn, until months later, from Dad, who had heard from Muffy, that they were living in New York. He would send money to Markie via Muffy but Markie's whereabouts were held secret by Muffy.

I would not see my brothers for another three years. I chose to lose my mother, but I did not choose to lose my brothers. During most of those three years I assumed my father knew very little about Markie's whereabouts or existence with my brothers, although I imagined he sent her money regularly via Muffy. I had a constant fear that Dad would suddenly announce, on any given day, that she was coming again, just as she had in Texarkana and in Boston, and that I would be forced to go see her. I will never know if Dad knew where she was her during that whole time.

Just being in Granny's house was some solace for the absence of my brothers. It was the biggest house I had ever seen. In fact, until then, I had never lived in a house. Life had been apartments in New York, Texarkana and Hagerstown. Life had been at most four rooms with a view of the sky or the street with no trees in sight. Granny's house was magnificent.

Seventy Centre Street stood out among the other houses on the Street. It was the only one painted a rich dark British racing green with black shutters. Four acres of lawn stretched to the right and back as you faced the house from the street. The lawn on the right bordered Voses Lane, named for a military hero of the town. Out back, Granny had planted peach and pear trees from which she regularly made peach ice cream and pear jelly. Out front on either side of the entrance to the driveway were two large stones painted white and marked with the number 70 in green that matched the color of the house. A stone wall hugged the front lawn and wound around down Voses Lane. The front door was black like the shutters and probably ten feet wide. Just inside to the far left, passed a small sitting room where Granny met with her widowed lady friends, was a large, covered, screened-in porch that had once been a library. The sun poured in on all three sides of the enclosed space, and you could roll down the green and white striped awnings when there was too much glare. It was a great place to play "jacks" when it rained in the summer because the little ball would bounce high on the wooden floors and you could listen to the rain while trying to beat the pants off your cousin. It was also a great place to be alone and to read.

Visitors who frequented Granny's house and enjoyed her hospitality were greeted by a large open foyer opposite the grand staircase. The wallpaper was light grey, covered in patches of black and white fleur de lis that formed a repeating pattern. Half way up the staircase on the first landing was a large walnut hope chest that smelled of camphor all year round and was filled with light white wool blankets for light bedding on cool summer nights.

In the eaves under the stairs on the first floor was a large black grand piano that filled the space in front of the living room. At night my father drank his pitcher of martinis and sat down to play "When They Begin the Beguine," the only song he remembered from years of piano lessons in childhood before sports became the focus of his life. He had relearned the song during his days in Texarkana. Strains of "When they Begin the Beguine" could be heard almost nightly, as my father plunked out the single notes of the melody with his right hand. With his left he sipped his martini.

Behind the piano there was a downstairs lavatory next the light-filled kitchen on one side. Granny had been smart enough to make this room into a communications center so that my cousin Edie and I could talk on the phone to friends without disturbing the nightly news programs that Granny loved to watch.

On the other side of the lavatory was a tiny hallway that led to a mudroom out back. The mudroom was the signature room of the whole house. Along the whole of one side of the room were glass-filled book cases descended to meet big heavy oak drawers filled with Roberts's memorabilia, clothes and sports equipment of every size and shape. Granny Roberts was nothing if not organized. In the glass cabinet shelves she had placed neatly, stacked foot-high piles of skirts and blouses, T shirts, socks and sweaters passed along by cousins who had outgrown them. In the drawers were varying styles and sizes of shoes, each pair tied together with a little tag attached that read "Teddy size 4 boys" or "Rachel size 6 dancing school" or "cleats—girls up to size 7." Across from the cabinets on big brass hooks hung enough sports equipment to field teams in baseball, hockey and soccer. A heavy laundry rope ran through the open parts of a catcher's mitt, a first basemen's glove, an outfielder's mitt and a catcher's mask, then tightly secured to one of the brass hooks. There were pairs of women's fancy ice skates hanging on the wall with the white polish worn off tied together with their sizes neatly marked, and black leather boy's hockey skates, and knee pads and shin guards. Every one of Granny's grandchildren would be well equipped to be safe during a game. In the corner behind the door stood old field hockey sticks, baseball bats and varying lengths of ice hockey sticks for competitive school sports. All raveled up at the other end of the room was a badminton net standing next to a croquet set missing two balls. The badminton racquets were with the tennis racquets that had been placed in their own category for safekeeping in one of the upper glass shelves next to the clothing.

The living room was a solid warm yellow, no wallpaper flowers here, with red leather bound books along the back wall to the right of the piano. In the middle of the room, opposite the bookcase, stood a black and white TV with rabbit ears on a small stand. The far wall had three large windows that let in jets of light in the late afternoon. Aunt Sis played bridge next to the windows with her great friends Bunny, Betsy and Kay from three o'clock until dinnertime many days of the week. At night Granny Roberts donned her nightly uniform of a navy blue cashmere sweater, blue jean skirt and pearls to watch Walter Cronkite, smoke cigarettes and drink her sherry.

To the right of the foyer was a dining room that could accommodate large family gatherings on holidays. Beyond the dining room a small pantry harbored all the silver and dishes for fancy dinners. It opened into a large kitchen, framed by a wall of windows on two sides that that looked out on the small tool shed we made into a doll house near the peach and pear trees.

Granny Roberts' interest in producing great Sunday lunches was renowned among the cousins, aunts and uncles. Granny would start early in the week by making peach ice cream from the peaches in the orchard behind the house. She would whip heavy cream with the peaches that had been finely chopped. She added the sugar and spun the whole pink mess in the Mixmaster. Then she took out the inner fillers from two ice cube trays and froze the newly minted ice cream in the trays for the end of the week.

On Sunday morning, Granny and I, but no one else, because no one else cared to, went to Saint Michael's, the Episcopal Church in town. Before going, early in the morning she peeled the potatoes and onions to surround the roast beef. Just before we left for the 11 am service, she popped the roast in the oven and set the time. We left church right after the first verse of the recessional ended, in order to get home in the time for the roast beef to still be rare. There would be broccoli to go with the golden roasted potatoes and the caramelized onions. But the best part, the piece de resistance of granny's culinary skills, was the Yorkshire pudding. She folded the batter over the roasting pan with a skill like no other. We loved to watch her. She would even add a little sherry from her glass to the gravy. Sunday lunch was a sacred ritual, like having a second communion of the day.

The house had three floors and a basement with a root cellar. The second floor had four bedrooms and three full baths. The bathtubs were amazing for their long length and porcelain curves. At times the three girl cousins took baths together in the long tub and sat for hours talking about American Bandstand or the new Beatles on the Ed Sullivan Show.

The bedrooms on the second floor were large and airy and each had a different color of flowered wallpaper. In every one there was a Queen Anne walnut bonnet- topped high chest made in nearby Salem, Massachusetts. I occupied a front room facing the yard which was pink and airy and had a closet the size of a small bedroom itself into which I regularly slept walked in the first few months I lived in the house as an unsure newcomer.

A dumbwaiter rose from the basement to the third floor, where my dad had created his own suite of rooms previously occupied by maids while he was growing up. A suite of three bedrooms and a bath with a skylight reached up to a fake widow's walk on the tiled roof. Two of the bedrooms were filled with "costumes." These were really petticoats Granny had worn when she was young, dresses from balls she attended in her youth and even costumes from old shows she had participated in as a member of the Vincent Club. There was even a Scottish kilt made over to be a drill costume with a black jacket, with silver buttons down the middle and festive epaulets with tassels on each shoulder.

Even then, as I played among the petticoats with my cousins, I displayed a theatrical bent that destined me to become a Vincent Show Girl like my mother and grandmother. I frequently engaged my cousins in amateur versions of "Gone with the Wind." I was always Scarlett. Little did I know that the young Vivien Leigh who played Scarlet on the big screen suffered from many of the same problems as my own mother. Cousin Rachel was Melanie, that sweet character who died in the end of the movie. She grew up to become a psychologist, married a psychiatrist and sings in a rock band with her husband. Cousin Joe, whose real name was Roger, who played the part of Rhett Butler, wore the jacket with the epaulets. He was smarter than all the rest of the cousins, chubby and looked nothing like the character in the film played by Clark Gable. Cousin Edie took the male role of the weak-willed Ashley Wilkes, who married Melanie before she died in child birth. Sometimes she wore the black jacket or borrowed one from my Dad's closet next door.

In the back of the house was a tool shed we called the "dollhouse" because we would sometimes move our play acting outdoors to this one room stage. On one occasion I buried guinea pig beside it that I had insisted on buying at the pet store with Dad's help but had quickly ignored. Next to the shed was a three car garage that housed the black 1949 Plymouth sedan that my father had driven to Texas and back, and a 1950 gray Studebaker that belonged to a woman named, Joan, a friend of my father's whom I had not yet met. The "putting green" was a loose term for what my father made out of a patch of grass in the middle of the driveway where cars drove in and turned around to drive out. He put a hole right in the middle of the patch, mowed the grass to a close cropped length, planted a stick in the hole and regularly worked on lowering his handicap in the evening.

Even at seventy Granny Roberts loved her daily dose of politics and media. She was strong and could be ornery with those who did not agree with her taste or her politics. All during the spring Edie and I had to fight to watch American Bandstand because Granny wanted to watch the McCarthy hearings in the late afternoon before cocktail time. I am not sure but had she lived a bit longer I think she would have voted for Adlai Stevenson and Estes Kefauver in the 1956 Presidential election. One thing I knew she, like the rest of the family, did not like the Kennedys, no matter what their party affiliation.

In the town next to Milton, Mattapan, there was a tailor named Gutman. He was Jewish and came to Boston from Russia after World War II. He joined Saint Michael's Church in Milton which Granny Roberts attended and became a devout Episcopalian. This turn of events improved both his English and his business. Granny was determined to have this man "fashion" my clothes in preparation for school in the fall. I would attend the fifth grade at the Charles Sumner Pierce Elementary School, aptly named for Granny's older brother. The school was more accurately named for the whole Pierce family, because the Pierces at one point owned and operated the oldest chocolate factory in America located in Milton. Granny wanted me to dress in a manner befitting that of her deceased brother, my great uncle.

I'm not sure whether it was the fitting for the pink- linen Bermuda shorts or the uncool plaid wool coat with the green velvet collar that sent me over the edge on a hot afternoon in July.

"Nobody wears shorts like that. Or that color. Those are for old ladies. I am NOT going to wear those!" I shouted at Granny trying unsuccessfully not to raise my voice in front of Mr. Gutman.

"Young lady, those shorts are best suited to your figure at this time and you are going to wear them."

"That coat looks like it belongs on an armchair. My friends would never wear that!" I said.

"What friends?" Granny asked in that cold, logical, low voice. "You haven't even gone to school here yet, so you don't know who your new friends will be."

"I assure you your new friends will like, even wear, shorts like these."

Maybe she had a point. Maybe she was looking out for me. Maybe there were things she knew that I didn't know about my new environment. In truth, I worshipped my Granny Roberts. When we arrived in Milton, Granny had just turned seventy. Although she had seen me as an infant, I had no prior recollection of her except for Markie's reference to her when she told my father to go home to his mother with his neckties.

Granny was an impressive figure. She had a full head of white hair, with a bluish tint left by a consistently careless hairdresser. She wore a white hairnet over her carefully coiffed "bob." At first I thought she had been born with white hair, until she told me she went white before her first child was born. She attributed her prematurely blanched state to a lack of B vitamins as a young woman. Built straight as an arrow, she moved about the house with swift grace all day long, forever, seeming to me, happily busy. Granny was a full five feet ten inches tall and just an inch shorter than my father, who often would not admit he was less than six feet tall. Dad could be vain, but Granny was always "razor-sharp and truthful."

At age ten I was in deep need of some tough love and straight talk. In a way, up to that point I had lost two mothers: the real one whom I did not wish to see, and Vada, who so ably and lovingly had cared for me in my mother's absence. This new person in my life was stronger than my mother, more direct, more of a guide for my life, and even argued with me from time to time. But always, through every conversation, I knew she loved me and was looking after me in a way no others could.

Granny was born in 1883, the product of her father's second marriage after being widowed. Her father, Edward Lillie Pierce, had six children with his first wife, Elizabeth Kingsbury, of Providence before she died in 1880. In 1882 he married Maria (pronounced ma-riah) Louisa Woodhead of Huddersfield, England. Grace Elizabeth, my grandmother, was the first of two children, followed by Harold Whitworth several years younger, who became a distinguished Bostonian and philanthropist in later life.

In her early twenties Granny married James Adams Roberts from the neighboring town of Dorchester. Although Granny may have married young, she was twenty-eight before the birth of her first child, Martha Lillie Roberts in 1911. She bucked her doctor's instructions to have no more because of a chronic heart condition and went on to produce five more before 1920. Her husband died one weekend of a mysterious illness when my father was eleven. Ultimately, Harold Whitworth Pierce would fund the educations of all six of Granny's children after she was widowed, and even put the boys through college.

Granny died two years after we moved to Milton, in February of 1956. My once vital and lively grandmother spent two years withering away from the ravages of colon cancer in the front bedroom on the second floor. Dad hoped for a cure for Granny's cancer. Always optimistic, but often, perhaps, in denial as he also thought his wife might one day be well.

At the time, children were generally shielded from knowing too much about death. I could hear Granny every night, sick as she was, getting up to go back and forth to the bathroom we shared. *Yea though I walk through the valley of the shadow of death, yet I will fear no evil.* I was not allowed to attend the funeral. I never got to say good bye to the best, most grand, mother of all.

Before she died Granny chose to leave me a piece of her that I will always treasure. In her will she bequeathed me some of the most beautiful silver ever seen anywhere. Three initials adorn every piece: GPR, Grace Pierce Roberts. A twelve piece setting for lunch and a twelve piece setting for dinner with the larger knives and forks for the evening meal. There are fish knives and grapefruit spoons and cake forks and butter knives for each place setting. The pattern is Fairfield and was sold by Shreve, Crump and Low, Boston's finest jeweler. I inherited the whole kit and caboodle with no pieces missing.

Granny invented "tough love" before it became popular. She was a trooper until the end. She died slowly, privately, painfully. Even at the last, she loved her pearls, her blue uniform, Walter Cronkite and me.

Two Schools of Thought

Fall 1954

In the fall of 1954, just before I entered the fourth grade, Granny was still alive then, and her connection to my new school intrigued me and made me proud. There, emblazoned in chrome letters high above the double front doors of the single story red brick building was Charles Summer Pierce Elementary School, named for my grandmother's brother. The architecture cried out "little red school house" of the early fifties.

On the first day of classes, as my father dropped me off in the circle outside the front door, he again reminded that we had a deep connection to this place I was about to enter. "That's Pierce, like an earring, not Perce, as the other side of our family pronounces it," my father reminded me. The fifth grade crossing guard greeted me as I stepped out of the car: "Hey, you're new here, where did you come from?" *New York, Texas, Maryland? Which was the right answer?* "I'm from here. The school's named after my great uncle."

"Oh, yeah, who says so?" replied the rough speaking woman with the badge. I didn't want to cause trouble and moved on not wanting to engage with her.

Mr. Silver was my fourth grade homeroom teacher. Early on I took note of the kind of clothes he wore. They did not look like my father's tweed suits that came from Brooks Brothers. They were monochromatic: one day a moss green suit with a matching green shirt and tie; the next day a brown synthetic with a toffee shirt and a chocolate string tie. A year later when I saw "Guys and Dolls" for the first time, I realized how much Mr. Silver looked like Frank Sinatra in the film. His thick jet black hair was always slicked back with much more than a dab of Brylcreem. *I dreamed last night I got on the boat to Heaven, and by some chance I had brought my dice along...* Mr. Silver looked like a bookie or a used car salesman and thought he was cool. I didn't.

Mr. Silver selected me to read "The Owl and the Pussy Cat" over the loudspeaker in the principal's office for an upcoming fall morning assembly. His reasoning was that I deserved a reward for reading the most books over the previous summer before school and receiving the most number of sticker stars beside my name on the honor roll of reading. I didn't see it that way. I was so scared that I pleaded sick on the appointed day and did not come to school. Mr. Silver knew I pulled a fast one and surprised me the next week by telling me I had to read it, this time without ever giving me a warning. Nice guy? I did not think he should ever have children, for fear of scaring them to death.

That same year my cousin Edie got breasts. This was a big deal for me. I still lived with Edie and Aunt Sis and Granny. Edie was in the sixth grade at the Academy. I was jealous of Edie in many ways and was not one to let competition defeat me. Edie went to private school. I went to public school. Edie's birthday was in March when all her friends could celebrate with her in school. Mine was in August when no one was around to give me presents. Edie was an only child and got lots of presents at Christmas. I had two brothers living with a mom in New York whom I never saw. Edie was taller than I, blond, blue-eyed, pretty and thin. I was short, chubby, and dark-eyed and had a bowl hair cut with bangs I never asked for. And to top things off, I had to wear Edie's "hand- me-downs" and those foul clothes from Mr. Gutman. But the main thing was Edie had breasts and I didn't.

I imagined that if I had a mother in my life she would say: "don't be ridiculous, you're too young to have breasts. You don't need to have breasts now. You have your whole life ahead to have breasts." But there was no one there. I couldn't ask my father, because I didn't think he would know about these things. I couldn't ask Aunt Sis, because, after all, she was the mother of Edie, who was the object of my jealousy.

I decided to have breasts, too. I got one of Edie's training bras out of her drawer when she had gone to school before me one day. With Edie out of the house, I stole her best bra. I put one pair of rolled up socks in the left cup and one in the right, hitched myself up and trotted off to school.

"Alright, hand them over" I heard Mr. Silver say without an ounce of doubt that I might actually have had the real things. This announcement did not come at a quiet moment or even during recess: it came during math

class. Another cause for a real embarrassment in front of my classmates, like the day my eye patch at the Rudolph Steiner School was exposed as a fake in first grade. Maybe this was another of my attempts at getting attention. It was certainly another reason to hate Mr. Silver.

It may sound lofty, but that fall, in addition to enrollment at the Pierce School I was introduced to the mores of two other institutions: the Episcopal Church and "dancing school."

There were lessons to be learned from both.

If Mr. Silver hadn't taken them away, I would definitely have worn those breasts to the first dance class and to church. I started going to church and dancing school at about the same time that year. The members of the dancing class were not my classmates yet. They were the fourth and fifth graders at the Academy. In church, however, there were kids from other schools, as well as my school, and the Academy. At church the message was that it doesn't matter who you are, you are welcome. *Let not the hope of the poor be not taken away.* Although it was fun, at dancing school I clearly sensed it mattered who you were and what private school you attended.

The dancing school was really only a rented space in the ballroom of a local private country club, named for some Massachusetts Indian tribe that no longer existed by the time the club was built. The classes were held on Friday afternoons, because the Academy had half-day classes that day so that older student athletes, mainly boys, could board busses to be driven to team matches played against other local private schools, while the younger kids could go to dancing school. No one's mother worked. So all mothers were free to attend games, help out with after game teas for team athletes or watch their children learn the foxtrot. I got special absence permission on Fridays from Mr. Silver to leave at noon to get ready for dancing class. Mr. Silver frowned on dancing school and referred to it as "a low form of sport."

Mrs. Brown, "Beanie" to her friends, most of whom were the parents of the dancing school students, was a tall, stout, jovial dance teacher, with a booming husky smoke-laden voice, a whiskey laugh, a sexy smile and a finer sense of rhythm in her tiniest baby finger than most people have in their entire body. That woman could dance. And she didn't care if her partner was nine years old or ninety, male, female or feline. She made everyone she came in contact with feel like a real dancer. She waved her fat hands, punctuating the air with the rhythms of whatever the sad eyed accompanist played on the upright piano in the back of the ballroom, and invited us to dance, dance, dance!

My older cousins, Joe and Edie, and younger cousins, brothers Peter and Jimmy Roberts attended dancing school with me. We formed our own Roberts family club within the contingent of about 30 budding ballroom dancers. In the beginning, I danced with stiff moving, towheaded boys in blue jackets who looked at the ceiling, anywhere but at me. At the start of each dance a new partner, chosen for me by Mrs. Brown, held his right arm and hand up, outstretched and in proper tilt to begin the box step or the waltz. I was far less shy than any of my young male counterparts. My father joked with me when he came to pick me up after the Friday afternoon sessions: "Be sure you don't lead your partner on the dance floor. Men are supposed to lead you." Somehow I never got the message on or off the dance floor. Little boys are basically afraid of little girls—for life.

In the spring when the yellow forsythia returned, I was truly bored of those Friday afternoons and longed to be outside on the club tennis courts. Fortunately, the advent of spring meant that the costume party would soon be scheduled for the last dancing class of the year.

The day of the party arrived. My cousin Joe sported a real Scottish kilt, with white leather knee britches that ran down his thighs and attached to some shiny black Brooks Brothers patent leather pumps that my father lent him. "Too bad I don't have a real cod piece to give you." I thought that has something to do with a dead fish and didn't get the joke.

Cousin Edie came as a ballerina, of course, but was as bored with dancing school as I and tried to sit out many of the dances. Jimmy and Peter were pirates from the high seas, each wearing a different pair of red pajama bottoms rolled up beneath vests borrowed from their father, Uncle Jim. Black tee shirts, blue bandanas tied round their necks and patches over their right eyes and a fake sword tucked inside an enormous wide belt holding up the pajamas.

Unfortunately, my costume, like my street clothes, had been made by Mr. Gutman. That was the beginning of a big mistake. I was a fat little Dutch girl in a green skirt with an organdy apron that spread across my

118

ample little tummy and tied in the back. I had yellow braids made of wool yarn that Granny Roberts had bought to cover my dark brown hair and bangs. Mr. Gutman had made an organdy hat with sides that were held up by wires in the organdy so that they turned out and up in the Dutch fashion as shown in children's books. The wooden shoes were the real piece de resistance. This was Granny's act of love. Never mind that I couldn't dance in wooden shoes. She loved the whole outfit, but I was beyond humiliation.

By now, at the end of the year, the dancers held each other with confidence, far less stiffly and less far apart than when classes began the previous fall. When a boy held his partner to begin the "box step," he no longer felt he was holding up a cardboard mannequin with curls.

Mrs. Brown announced that she was introducing a new dance on this final day of class. The dancers formed couples and imagined a launch into the rhythms of Bill Haley's "Rock Around the Clock." Instead, what followed was a very athletic endeavor called the "Mexican Hat Dance." Mrs. Brown handed out huge colorful sombreros to each couple and instructed the boy partner to put on the hat. The hats were so big that, when the couples changed partners, the hats masked most of the boys' faces from the eyes of their next partner.

Mrs. Brown probably did not know the Mexican hat dance is actually a courting dance for grown- ups. In 1919, Russian Ballerina Anna Pavlova traveled to Mexico and instantly fell in love with the dance. She was so enamored with it that she added what she knew as the "Mexican Hat Dance" to the dance routines she performed around the world.

The original dance begins with a man flirting with a woman, trying to woo her. Eventually, he becomes cocky and the woman shoos him away. Finally, when he succeeds in wooing her, he throws his hat to the ground and kicks his leg up over the woman as she bends down to pick the hat. They continue to dance until the end, when they finally kiss.

Our little dance was no match for the flirting couples south of the border. The ornate skirts worn by the original women performing the dance were replaced by our thin little organdy laced tea dresses, The black suits decorated with silver buttons worn by the men in the dances during the 1930's were replaced by navy blue blazers with silver buttons and boys Brooks Brothers ties.

The piano player did his best to bang out the beat of the dance while Mrs. Brown accompanied with a pair of mariachis. At one point we do-si-doed around each other three times and then moved on to new partners giving the next boy his turn with the hat. No thought of the flirting Mexican young couples, we were just innocents at play.

Granny Roberts had taken me to church for the first time right before Thanksgiving. I was instantly hooked on church as soon as I heard the first strains of "We gather together to ask the Lord's blessing" and fell in love with "I sing a song of the Saints of God......and God help me to be one, too." I loved the ritual, the litany of the service though I didn't really understand much of it, and, most of all, the music. I believed, like the hymn, humans could be saints too, just like Granny Roberts.

Dancing school, on the other hand, offered another kind of ritual, a training ground for life. It instilled confidence and developed one's ability to move gracefully in all manner of social situations, to move easily from one partner to another and to be able to converse lightly with all manner of persons and personalities anywhere anytime. I was going to be a scholarship student at a private school the next year, but I was already prepared to fit in because I had been introduced ahead of time to Mrs. Brown's dancing class and to the open arms of the Episcopal Church.

Reunited for Good

In the fall of 1955 I entered Milton Academy. I was accepted partly because my father went there and partly, after already attending eleven schools in New York, Texas and Maryland I was adaptable and could be charming when I needed to be. I loved the school's motto: *Dare to be True.*

I made new friends, as Granny Roberts knew I would. I was living in a beautiful house with my dad and my grandmother who doted on me. There was no one else to divert their attention. Even my jealous feelings about my cousin Edie, who lived in the same house, took flight. Edie had her own group of friends, but now so did I, so our lives were comfortably parallel. It helped that she had gone on to the Upper School at Milton Academy while I was placed in the sixth grade of the Lower School. We mostly saw each other at home after school to watch American Bandstand.

None of the cousins knew where Markie and my brothers went after Markie stole them from that Boston hotel. Later, I would learn that they went to live in Brooklyn in one of those long narrow apartments known as a railroad flat. I will never know what Cam and Teddy endured in that period of their lives because, in fact, neither brother remembers a single day in their lives before they finally returned to Milton when Teddy was then nine and Cameron barely three years old. The reunion came about in a swift and unexpected way.

One day during the summer after my first year at Milton Academy I was on the front steps of 70 Centre Street with my cousins Edie and Joe and Jimmy and Peter. Not only did we do dancing school together but we loved to play softball, touch football and croquet, anything that helped spin off our considerable physical energies with some fun. The cousins moved out onto the lawn to set up badminton net in the front yard. Whitey, Edie's cat, was hanging out watching the Roberts clan. Joe and Peter were placing the poles that would hold up the net. Edie was unraveling the net and laying it out on the ground to get ready to lift onto the waiting poles. I sat on the porch watching all of this when my father bolted out of the front door. As he opened the outer screen I heard:

"They've found them."

I knew exactly what that meant, even though my cousins had no idea. Joe and Edie vaguely heard their Uncle George's words and went on putting the game together. I would never know whether my older cousins, Joe and Edie, knew where Teddy and Cameron were but didn't tell me, or if they didn't know. I was too afraid to ask. I was afraid, too, to ask Dad if he had been searching for my brothers or whether someone else found them and called him.

"They are in an air raid shelter in Queens. They have been there for three days and apparently would not give their names or the name of their mother who has disappeared and left them at the shelter. I guess Teddy finally gave his name and Markie's. I'm not sure. But I have got to go there." *Why was this the first time I had ever heard of any of this? Was I supposed to understand? Good for Teddy for coming forward!*

Right. Had she done it again? Had she tried to kill them, too? Did they run away? Did she run away from them? How did they get to a Civil Defense Air Raid shelter? What did the bomb shelter have to do with all of this? As my father left, I made myself rejoin the mindless game in front of me.

Thwack. Whack. The shuttlecock stuck in the net and I lost the point.

"You idiot! Did you do that on purpose?" Joe, who was a year older than I, way smarter, and big and heavy, had just served. I ran to the net to hit the white little plastic birdie with the rubber tip and I whiffed it just as it crossed the net. But I didn't really care about the insult or missing the shot.

My mind was not on the game. It was on my brothers. Were they coming to stay? Would my world be different? It had been so grand these past few years with just my Dad and Granny Roberts fulfilling most of my needy wishes and making me feel whole and, most of all, healthy. It was only sometimes now, infrequently, when I was at school, when I wondered if the other kids knew I was different from them, that my mom was "away." Did I look like someone whose mom had tried to get rid of her in a manic moment?

That night, as I did most nights, especially when my homework was done and before Dad would come in to kiss me goodnight, I played my records on the victrola. My favorite album was *Folk Songs of England and*

Wales. "The ash grove, the ash grove how quietly is sleeping; the ash grove the ash grove alone is my home..." So soothing, so peaceful, so simple, and so safe. Dad would not kiss me goodnight that night. He would not be there that night. He was in Brooklyn, New York. I didn't know what was coming. I prayed that all would go well for all of us and that Granny would live. Amen.

Once again, as in Maryland after Cameron was born, I need not have worried. Dad returned three days later just when he said he would. He arrived with Teddy in tow and Cameron in his arms. In the first few days we got to know each other all over again. I marveled at my two brothers whom I had not seen in three years. How quiet Cameron was in the little blue corduroy overalls and his little blue sweater. Both Teddy and Cameron had underpants stamped on the back with "property of Civil Air Raid Defense, Brooklyn, N.Y." Everywhere we went, Cameron held onto my right hand, always looking up at me, trusting I would pull him along with me wherever I went. It was the same with Teddy though he was bigger and more confident in his new surroundings.

It was great to be together again. Teddy was as sweet as ever. Because he missed entering the first grade until he was almost eight, my father put him into the Pierce Elementary School very soon after his arrival in Milton. Teddy was so proud to be in Granny's big house with the beautiful lawn out front that he invited some of his new classmates over to show them his fancy house.

One night, while he was playing the piano and sipping martinis, Dad called Teddy away from the TV over to the piano. "You know, Teddy, not everyone in Milton, or anywhere, for that matter, lives in a house like this. You could hurt a friend's feelings by taking them on a tour when they come here." My father asked Teddy what the apartment was like in Brooklyn. Teddy did not know. He could not remember anything before coming to his new home in Milton. This amnesia was stunning to me as I could all too easily and, and at times unnervingly, remember everything back to the age of two in Greenwich Village.

In a gentle tone and with much love, Dad told him to not show off in front of his friends or they might not be his friends for long. All three of us wanted to believe that our new life was real, that it was not going away, and that we were a part of something better than the craziness we had known together. Better that Teddy and Cameron could not remember or recount any of it. For some, pain has a way of making you numb and able to you forget. For me I found strength in remembering everything.

Harpy in the House

1958

At the time my father may have been struggling as a single parent, and as a son with a dying mother, quite by accident he found someone whom he felt could bring sanity and order into to his life and household. He was an easy mark for the recent divorcee from Saint Louis.

Joan Jacoby Scullin, my soon to be stepmother, and Markie Byron, my mother, were the same age and were in the same class for a time at Beaver Country Day school before my mother left for Miss Hall's school in the Berkshires of western Massachusetts.

While Markie's heritage was considered "patrician" for the times, Joan's was much more middle class. Some thought that Joan might be Jewish, because of her father's last name, Jacoby. These social differences would be reflected in the ways in which each would mock the other to me over my lifetime.

Joan's father was born in England. I'm not sure what he did for a living. I do know he became a hypnotist of sorts, attempting to assist the ill with his healing powers in his spare time. All I know about Joan's mother was that she was bedridden long before I met her. Early on, Joan told me that her mother's mother had escaped Boston by going west with Brigham Young, the founder of the Mormon Church, to Pike's Peak. Joan had two brothers. One wanted to become a pitcher for the Boston Braves. I don't know if that ever happened. The other, Ernest, became the head of a famous vocational school in Boston and married well. I was only in the sixth grade when I met Joan but even then I wondered if she had had, like me, very little mothering. Her mother's pain management required so much attention that Joan had been left alone a lot to figure things out. I wanted to like this woman.

Joan had two children: Matt was the same age as I and Jane was four years my senior. The kids remained in Saint Louis with their father when Joan first came east to her childhood home in Brookline to care for her

125

ailing mother, to wait for her divorce to be final and to find a job. Joan and my father met at a party on Saint Patrick's Day in 1956, a month after Granny's funeral, and by the following Monday Joan was hired as his fulltime personal assistant. They would marry in the fall of 1958 when Joan's children came to Milton to stay for good.

A lot happened between Joan's first hello and the wedding that took place in the Milton Academy chapel during my eighth-grade year. I was first introduced to Joan by my father at the home of one of his best friends. Joan must have asked Dad what I was like. Dad probably said I was smart and pretty well-adjusted for a child of divorce living with her father, her cousin and her aunt in Granny Roberts's big old house. Joan would have likely asked what size dress I wore. My father made the mistake of saying his daughter was pretty chubby for an eleven year old. This was the beginning of trouble.

At that first introduction Joan presented me with a blue and red cowgirl outfit: a matching skirt and shirt in Chubbette sized thirteen and a half. The red bandana that came with the outfit was meant to be tied around the neck so the wearer could look like Dale Rogers. "George tells me you like to dress up and pretend to be characters in movies and books. I thought you would enjoy this outfit because it's a little Western but you could wear it to school."

After a false and faint thank you, on the way home I told Dad "I will not be caught dead alone in my own bathroom in that outfit." I was not amused by the color, the look, shape and most of all the size of my two-piece cowgirl outfit.

I should have learned from our first meeting, but, like all first born children, I wanted to please. I wanted to be liked. I wanted to feel normal like other kids who had normal mothers who lived with their families. I had loved Granny Roberts but never wanted her to come on school visits with me because everyone would see how old she was and that she certainly wasn't my mother. Maybe they would know I didn't have a mother anymore. Not now. Not ever. But not Joan, either.

With Joan in the picture, my father's spirits lifted from his grief over his mother's recent death in February, 1956. Being a father of three children all of a sudden and all at once with the responsibility of running an expanding household was tough. He was a genuinely kind man who blanched at the thought of ever spanking a child, even when it might be called for. But he was no management guru on the domestic front. Joan was a wizard of an organizer with a heart of stone and a jealous ego the size of a small ocean. She was prepared to put my father's life and household in order under her command.

Dad was proud that his first child was attending the prep school from which he and his siblings had graduated. He hoped his sons would, too. Every morning, my father reviewed my French vocabulary homework with me although he spoke no French and pronounced every syllable badly. Then he got Teddy ready for school and made sure Cameron was with the Irish housekeeper, Mary Smith, who had taken care of all the cousins before we came along. In a way, it was becoming a tight-knit family, just the four of us, even without Granny. My father spent a lot of time teaching me how to throw a baseball like a man, how to skate like a hockey player and how to play tennis. My brothers liked sports, too, but were younger and less ready to rough it up. By now I even had my own subscription to *Sports Illustrated*. One day a boy in my class named John walked me home from school. On the table inside the front door was a copy of Sports Illustrated addressed just to me, to Diana Roberts, at 70 Centre Street, Milton, MA. A Christmas present from my dad that he no doubt wanted to share.

"Girls are not supposed to read that magazine. That's not right. You should not have that. That is so unladylike. Don't tell me you know all the stats in the National and American Leagues?" My father had ordered the magazine the Christmas before, so I had quite a lot of time to memorize them. Fully armed with the numbers myself, I was capable of alienating any boy I encountered in school, on the way home or on my own turf. Yet Dad stepped right up to the plate before I could start my own protest.

"John, Diana has been following the leagues for over a year now and we do quizzes like math tests every morning. Wanna try us?"

That was the end of my friendship with John. We had no quizzes and John never asked to walk me home again. Did Dad have an ulterior motive here? I was always his one and only girl and he my main man.

My father made good choices for his children: to live in a town like Milton close to family, to send us to good schools and to provide what he thought would be a stable home. In the words of the Milton Headmaster

Field's words he may have been "eminently reliable" but why did he so unreliably choose to marry a woman whom he knew early on had been hospitalized with a mental disorder? His mother's death hit him hard. He believed naively to the end that she would recover with the help of a not very good doctor who was a drinking buddy of the family. He continued to see Markie after the first divorce. When Cameron was born, he remarried Markie and then divorced again. What kind of decision maker was he? *What was he thinking? What was I thinking?* It pained me to be aware, as a teenager, of these thoughts about a man I loved so much.

Not long after the Dale Rodgers incident, Joan asked me to call her "mother" two years before my father and she would marry. I had never used that term even for my own birth mother so why would I welcome that offer? I don't know why but I did. When I learned that Joan was pregnant at the wedding ceremony in the late fall of 1958 I knew I had made a mistake. In my mind I rescinded the offer. From then on I referred to her as the *Harpy,* the predatory monster in the house. When my half sister, Lacy, was born retarded the following July, I asked myself if this was the will of the Greek Gods or the Christian God I had come to believe in?

The real irony here is that Markie and Joan had a common bond. They were the same age and in the same class in the same girls' school in Boston. But they were opposites from the first day their paths crossed in class. Where Markie may have been the aloof femme fatale, Joan was a flying buttress. Markie was the real deal, the rich girl; Joan was the original social climber always trying to fit into the in crowd. Joan said Markie was always crazy. Markie referred to Joan as "The Jewess." That remark turned out to be true and was the reason Joan was never asked to debut in Boston or to attend coming out parties.

Markie's family may have fallen on hard times during the depression and beyond but the gentility was always there. Even in madness Markie she spoke politely, slowly, in refined tones and delicate predicates. She said "how fabulous! "About the slightest little thing I or anyone said. When we were little, she smothered us with verbal love, until she couldn't. She knew to stay in the shade of life. Joan, on the other hand, lived in the hot burning sun and scorched us all with her fury, her verbal heat and crushing demands. The fire never seemed to go out.

Joan really did arrive as a full blown version of modern day Harpy. To me Joan was a fast flying creature with a hooked nose and clawing magenta fingernails that always left behind a loathsome stench sickening to all she encountered. The real Harpies, known as "the hounds of Zeus," would swoop down and defile food, leaving it so foul that no one could bear to be near it, much less eat it. I knew a live Harpy had come into my life to stay.

In 1939, the then young Joan Jacoby had just turned twenty. Too poor to go to college, Joan was working at the 1939 World's Fair when she met and later married a man from Saint Louis. Joan had two children before she decided, in 1956, that it was time to divorce her husband, due to his drinking habits and that fact that he had had an affair. It also happened that Joan's mother, a widow who had been bed ridden for many years, needed her back home.

From the outset, as a stepmother, Joan was verbally combative, on the offensive and extremely competitive and unrelentingly protective of her relationship with my Dad. As it turned out, she liked me the least of her three stepchildren because my father favored me. To me, she was all tight skirts, big boobs and heavy makeup, with streaks of blond and black hair and fluorescent magenta lips with fingernails to match. On afternoons when I arrived home from school she would bark: "Get the hair out of your eyes, you look like a slut!" Given the occasion, I would have returned the compliment.

Joan was always going on diets, starving herself, while making high-calorie, high-carb "treats" for the rest of us that she couldn't eat herself. If I thought I had hated American gravy and hamburgers earlier in my life, now I turned my nose up at spaghetti and sauce and her chocolate Yule log which she made year round not just at Christmas. One of her favorites was German chocolate cake with cocoanut frosting.

One night I was convinced that Joan had made the German Chocolate cake to test her will power as well as mine. She often alluded to my teenage *avoir du pois* but never offered to diet with me. I think she liked to compare her discipline with my lack of will. Late in the evening I snuck down the back stairs to the kitchen. With silence and great care I scraped the outside of the cake, building a mound of frosting on my index finger until it was the size of a large mouthful. I scooped it up into my mouth in one sweet bite. Then I cut the part of the cake that no longer had any frosting on its edge and pitched it into the garbage. I gave two more pieces the same treatment. After I scraped all the frosting off the top, the sides and the middle, I ate the smooth buttery frosting and threw away the cake. By midnight I knew I would be in trouble in the morning.

"You have made five housekeepers leave, but you are goddamn not going to make me leave, do you hear," she yelled at me picking the cake pieces up out of the garbage. "I made that cake for you and your brothers, and now look what you have done!"

Teddy would only eat chicken noodle soup and egg salad sandwiches he made for himself and little Cameron. New stepbrother Matt was used to his mother's cooking from Saint Louis and didn't know the difference between fresh spaghetti and ravioli or the canned version. Dad had so many martinis in the pitcher he made every night that he didn't care what he ate. I guess I was the only one who acted out against Joan's outbursts. Often I retreated to the porch and sat alone outside for hours until the coast was clear and the Harpy and Dad went to bed.

After the wedding we moved to a new house about a mile from 70 Centre Street following the distribution from Granny Roberts' will. Every day for the next several months of that spring there were verbal battles, mostly because Joan was pregnant and irritable. One day in the spring, while rummaging through my parents' bedside table for a pair of scissors, I found a note in a small white envelope addressed in typed letters to me. I opened it carefully so as to be able to reseal it as if it has not been opened. It read:

> Diana:
> I regret to inform you that I fear you are or will be as crazy as your mother. You behavior is so strange of late. Your father and I do not understand you and worry about you. Please do something about this.
>
> Joan
> Like what? Kill myself so you can have my father all to yourself?

There were also my two new siblings, Joan's children, to contend with. Matt was put into Class IV at the Academy which was also my class. Jane

went to another school. From the start Matt was a problem for me. First off all, one by one, my previous girl friends became his. Like the work of a serial killer, my friends disappeared from walks home or weekend sleepovers. It didn't seem fair. An entry in my diary at the time read:

Dear Cassandra:

They say that love is closely allied with hate. Therefore I cannot find the words to accurately describe what I feel for my stepbrother. He is impossible. I detest him odiously – and contemptuously. He is avaricious and doesn't know his own mind when given a responsible task. Maybe I am jealous, but I always thought that jealousy came in the form of: "Oh, gee, I wish I could be like that person, why can't I?"

Joan would be married to my father for less than a decade before he passed away that Christmas while I was in the Peace Corps. She went on to marry three other men before passing away in her late eighties. A year after my father died, she married a classmate of my father's named John and moved to Atlanta. A year later she divorced him, because he became a drunk. She put a personal ad in the **Atlantic Monthly** that resulted in her fourth husband, an advertizing executive who had retired to Saskatchewan. Joan then discovered a much older man who had been one of the inventors of the early UNIVAC computers. They married and lived in Princeton, New Jersey. In the end she found money, respectability and someone who could take care of her and Lacy for the rest of their lives.

The Message
in Filene's Basement

1958

Milton Academy was founded in 1798. Just short of a century later, it was discovered that the school was entitled by law to have a seal, which of course meant it must have a motto. Seventeenth Century poet George Herbert's principal work, a long series of poems called "The Temple" served as the source the school's emblematic motto:

"The stormy working soul spits lies and froth.

Dare to be true. Nothing can need a lie."

High School was a series of bumps and bruises for me, beginning with the fall of 1958. The Milton motto lurked in the back of my mind whenever I started to wonder why life was taking a certain turn to or away from my teenage aspirations.

For some time I had been wondering why my parents seemed to have enough money to spend on liquor but never enough for a bicycle or a summer vacation. Any money I had I earned babysitting on weekends and in the summer. None of us had a weekly allowance.

One Friday afternoon, after school was let out, I walked from my house to the trolley in Milton Village wearing a plaid skirt, white blouse with brown knee socks and loafers, perfectly, properly put together. I was not allowed to ride the subway or go to school in pants or blue jeans. Joan picked out this skirt, mixed brown and green, two colors I hated and I thought were reserved for color blind men who couldn't see the difference. I rode the trolley to Ashman station where I caught the Red Line to the retail district in Boston.

Riding alone on the subway, I noticed a number of mothers and daughters who were probably headed in the same direction as I for an afternoon of shopping. Joan and I never shopped because she was always busy, at first working for my Dad, and later busy with Lacy. I didn't mind.

But I did mind when she brought home those ugly *Lenz* dresses or those dirndls that made me look like a German milkmaid looking for a guy in lederhosen. Although I had never shopped with my own mother, I often recalled that she would order socks from department stores that would be oversized so that I might grow into them. I folded the socks over my toes to make them fit snugly into my Buster Brown boys' shoes. It felt almost like having bound feet Chinese style. To this day my toes curl over and I have tiny feet.

There has never been a marketplace like the original Filene's Basement. It was more like a Paris flea market. There were pastel-colored sweaters everywhere in different sizes and lined canvas bins set out on the floor with discount signs hanging on strings overhead. Swimsuits marked down to one-fifth of the original designer named price were displayed on makeshift counters. There were even special "designer's rooms" with Chanel and other high end suits and cocktail dresses. The signature event of the year was the famed race for bargains by young women buying their wedding gowns in the "Basement."

I looked at several pairs of khaki shorts after passing up the lighter pastel versions. I passed the shoe rack and the section with all the stockings I was not yet permitted to wear, except at dancing school or at one of the several dances called "Sociables" during the school year. I hated the garter belts that held them up.

I spotted the shirt on top of a small cardboard bin. Ironically, it was covered in gold and brown circles representing coins the size of half-dollars or quarters. The shirt was made of cotton but sturdier with three buttons down the front so that the owner could pull it on overhead and let it hang outside a skirt or pair of pants. It was three in the afternoon and not crowded in the shirt and blouse department.

The shirt was actually inside a plastic bag on top in the bin with other less colorful shirts in size twelve. Never even looking around to see who might be watching, I stuffed the shirt inside my coat into the big pocket just below my left shoulder. Price $14.95. I didn't understand why I felt so good at the time, full of adrenaline and an immediate sense of accomplishment.

I stayed around to look at pajamas and bathrobes for another fifteen minutes and then walked casually back up the basement stairs to the street level to take the subway back to Ashmont and the trolley home with my new shirt.

"How could you do this?" the Harpy shrieked at me while holding the gold shirt over my head as I was waking up.

"What? Where did you get that?" I asked, becoming indignant at the violation of my privacy.

"In your bottom drawer while I was cleaning your room," Joan continued, more exercised with each utterance from her huge chartreuse mouth.

"You never clean my room! What right did you have to come in here? This is my room."

"This may be your room, young lady, but this is my house and you are going to turn yourself in for this theft and earn the money to pay for this shirt. I have already spoken to the Filene's basement floor walker. He will see you next Saturday at three on the floor."

This was Saturday afternoon when Joan confronted me, the time when I was supposed to clean my room and change the sheets. Once she closed the door, I lay down on my bed in the unchanged sheets and did not move for several hours. I didn't even think about the consequences of my actions. I was just plain mad that Joan had entered my room, my bureau and my life, violating me with her stepmother commando authority.

I took the train into Boston the following Saturday. I did not wear my parka. This time I wore my longer Sunday coat that had no pockets. I carried the shirt in an unmarked brown paper bag. Luckily, Joan had not told the headmistress at school about my criminal activity. Although she might have liked to, it was just too embarrassing. I have no recollection of Dad's role in this event.

"What is a nice girl from a prep school doing stealing clothes she does not need?" I heard the floor walker bark as I stood in front of him and several surrounding sales clerks. Neither I nor the floor walker knew the answer to that question. I could feel a noose being thrown over my head, tightening its grip on me, an albatross hanging from my neck. Fear and shame were rendering me speechless before the unwitting employees who now turned their attention to the floor walker and me.

Three months and fifteen babysitting hours later I returned the full price of the shirt to the floor walker at Filene's Basement. But in the end I also got something from Filene's more valuable than what I had stolen. I

found out how painful dishonesty can be. It's not worth the risk and the consequence of an albatross. *Dare to be true.*

The Filene's "incident" proved to be just one of many indications that I might not be ready for a straight four year ride through college after high school. By senior year the headmistress of the Academy told me I was too immature to actually succeed in a larger universe. Although outwardly I put on a good face, inside I had completely shut down emotionally for those last four years. In addition, Joan made it clear to me that my father couldn't afford to send his oldest child to college anyway. If she hadn't been able to go to college, why should I? With Joan there was always a competition or an agenda on some level, hidden or unhidden. While I was losing ground and getting into trouble, others in my class seemed to thrive.

Head Mistress

My feelings of being more and more an outsider increased with each advancing year of high school. Two incidents determined the measure of my time at Milton Academy. Both of them involved a woman whose name still brings fear and loathing to half of every class of girls whose academic future she determined.

In 1949, the Trustees of Milton Academy appointed a new woman to succeed the venerable Miss Faulkner as Headmistress of the Girls' Upper School. The choice was a twenty- nine old, Radcliffe graduate who had majored in French. It is commonly thought she became a private school administrator following a failed romance that ended her engagement to a Harvard man.

Failed romances were routinely attributed to single unmarried teachers who came to Milton over the years. There was Miss Howard, our Class V home room teacher, who chain smoked, had thin curly blond hair, was muscular and wiry and wore gray masculine jackets and three quarter length skirts. We taunted her by crawling under our desks during class time when we were supposed to be studying A Tale of Two Cities. Then there was Miss Lawry, the beautiful, rosy-cheeked English teacher who was six feet tall and had such a big rear end that we were sure she would never find anyone to marry her. Her brother was the Episcopal Bishop of Massachusetts. He came to Saint Michael's Church each year to celebrate with those of us who had completed confirmation classes. He was even taller than his sister, handsome and rugged as a soldier. What was appealing in his looks seemed homely and awkward in Miss Lawry. We felt sorriest of all for the two gym teachers who lived quietly together as a couple at the edge of the Milton campus. Miss Barry and Miss Stillman remained close for many years until Miss Stillman's death. It was said that poor Miss Stillman's fiancé "had died in the Great War." Later, much later, I realized that they were a brave and happy couple in a time when those "partnerships" were unacceptable in most sectors, save perhaps in the secluded world of private schools.

When the trustees hired the new headmistress, they decided she was so inexperienced that she should travel the country for a year before her tenure began in order to gain knowledge of the best practices in private secondary girl's school education. The education and personal philosophy she put together in the coming years would impact the lives of many young girls between 1950 and 1981 and scar some with psychological trauma.

The spring of 1958 marked the end of my eighth grade year and after that and Dad's remarriage, over the summer, things begin to deteriorate at home. Joan became increasingly dictatorial, and I became sullen and stubborn. On my birthday in August, when Dad and Joan presented me with gifts and a cake, I refused to eat the cake and insisted on opening the presents alone and away from anyone. I offered no thanks for the gifts, and that night went out in back of the house and sat for hours on a pile of dirt that had been excavated to make way for a paved garage space. I cried long and hard, not knowing why I was so unhappy and felt so alone.

I came inside from the dirt pile around midnight to find the cake in the kitchen and presents neatly placed together beside the cake on the kitchen table. My Dad was sitting there still sipping his martini. His head was slightly tilted, his face red and his eyes watery. His shaggy grey Shetland sweater that covered his Brooks Brothers shirt was worn full of holes, and he was sitting at the table in his boxer shorts. This was his nightly uniform and routine.

"Hi, sweetheart, where have you been? I know it wasn't the best of birthdays. But we can take a spin tomorrow night. Maybe go to the Dairy Queen. Put a smile on your face. I can't stand it when you don't smile. It breaks my heart." My heart was breaking, too.

The one bright spot in my life that kept me out of the house and away from Joan's clutches was my first summer job. I was a camp counselor in the Italian section of Boston, the North End, where every day I rode a yellow bus filled with young, poor Italian kids to various parks and outdoor sights in and around Boston. The Fresh Air Camp took inner city kids to Nantasket Beach, Fenway Park, museums, outdoor swimming pools and the movies. For a kid who was too poor herself to have a summer place and couldn't stand being stuck at home, this was heaven.

Every day while we rode the bus to and from our outings, I stood at the head of the bus and engaged the kids in silly or familiar songs. My favorite was complete nonsense:

"I'm up here in the nut house; my mind is in a rut.

My teacher thinks I'm cuckoo but he is off his nut.

Oh, looped-diloop-in the noodle soup when the witches have a broom.

You can bake a steak or fry a cake when the mud pies are in bloom.

Do six and six make nine, does ice come from the vine.

Does ole black Joe come from Kokomo in the good old summer time?"

At the end of the day the kids and I would run in and out of the outdoor sprinklers the square in the North End and watch old men play chess or bocce as the afternoon sun faded and cooled down the day. Every day my dad drove me to the bus to greet the kids and picked me up after his work day at John Hancock to take me home. The car rides were everything to me and the best part of the day.

In the fall of 1958, Class IV began ominously. "The headmistress would like to see you in her office this afternoon." This request came from Miss Remick, the maiden aunt of movie star Lee Remick, who would win an Oscar for *The Days of Wine and Roses* with Jack Lemmon. She was so nice and unassuming I wondered why no man had scooped her up.

"So, Diana, how was your summer?" the headmistress began. "I heard that you worked in a camp for underprivileged children. That was very good of you." Silently I wondered what she could possibly know about underprivileged children since she had always known privilege

and had never known little children.

"Talking to your teachers this fall, I hear you are having a bit of a struggle. You know, when you came here in the sixth grade, we thought you were one of the smartest girls ever to be admitted. But now I must say that since your father remarried last spring we think you have become emotionally disturbed. We are going to take you out of the honors sections to take the pressure off you academically."

This bombshell rendered me speechless, stunned, confused and utterly without self-confidence. It didn't help that in late August, after my camp counselor job ended, my father informed me that Markie had asked for a visit and was planning to come on the train from New York to meet with Teddy, Cameron and me before school started. I assumed that my father and Markie no longer communicated, but now I wasn't so sure. Was there some right she had to seeing us? Were we legally in Dad's custody? No one told us and we didn't ask.

Already on shaky terms with my stepmother, I didn't have room in me to deal with another broken relationship. The albatross was circling low. I hadn't seen Markie since I was nine, when I watched her being carried out by force to an ambulance in a straight jacket. I never wanted to see that again. Nevertheless, I agree to go with my brothers to meet her in Boston for lunch and an afternoon visit.

Lunch in a Boston Diner

We walked together to Milton Village to ride the trolley to the subway leading into Boston. Cammy was nine, Teddy was twelve and I was, by then, fifteen. We were going to South Station to meet Markie's train from New York at noon on Saturday afternoon late in the summer of 1959. We mostly didn't talk as we marched toward the train station, apprehensive of what might be ahead. Teddy and Cam had last seen Markie screaming in that shelter like a caged animal, before she was handcuffed and led away by police to a quiet cell at Belleview. I wondered whether they had the same fear I did, but I didn't ask.

We stood on the platform, each of us trying to remember what Markie looked like or might look like now. Teddy and I recalled the chicken pox incident and how I broke Teddy's nose in the apartment in New York. We held hands and waited for the train to arrive.

"Hello, D-I-A-N-A, precious angel let me hug and hold you! And you, Teddy, you have lost all your curls, but how handsome you are! And Cammy, you look so much like your father. The resemblance is amazing. Let me hug all of you!"

Not really caring about where to eat or even wanting to be there that day, I decided on the restaurant nearest to the station at which we were able to get a table easily. Dad had given me a fair amount of money to pay for the lunch and the additional funds he knew Markie would be asking for. We settled on eating at a diner next to South Station. The restaurant was nothing like Howard Johnson's, my father's favorite restaurant for fried clams, chowder, brown bread and the 28 flavors of ice cream. Dad was a loyalist when it came to food. One of his favorite things to do was to make real lobster Newburg at home with sherry and freeze it until the right occasion came along to devour it with a few martinis. I knew Markie ate little, fretted over the nutrition of everything, so why bother to seek out a Ho Jo's on this day?

Sitting in the booth, I peered over my menu at my mother. The right corner of her mouth sagged and she kept sticking her tongue out and pulling it back like a desert lizard. I could tell her mouth was dry and she needed water every few minutes. We ordered hamburgers, but I noticed Markie was not interested in food when it was her turn to order.

"Babies, you need your strength. Order anything you want. Mashed potatoes are really good for you. Do you remember when we used to eat hamburgers and Franco American gravy? I tried so hard to make you healthy and smart."

Smart? I didn't know that was part of the equation. Was Markie smart? Could you be smart and crazy at the same time? Was I not smart and crazy at the same? What would the headmistress say?

"So, Markie, why did you not go to college? I am thinking about college now and feeling a little discouraged."

"Oh, darling, you don't need college. You are beautiful and talented, and some great young man will scoop you up." Then she added something I didn't need to hear:

"As Nat Clifford wanted to do with me-until he died, and then I married your father. Did I tell you he raped me on our first visit?" *Not again, not in front of my brothers.*

I had gotten pretty much the same answer about "no college" earlier from Joan. She said that she had not gone to college, but did study piano briefly one summer at Smith, and didn't think four years at any college necessary for me. Besides, my father couldn't pay for it.

"If not college, Markie, what did you want to do with your life?"

"Well, Diana, that's a hard question to answer." Markie's voice trailed off into silence. I could see and hear her rubbing fingers together agitatedly, not sure how to continue.

"I was not the college type, and in those days not many women went to college.

I became first a model for hands and then for jewelry and then hats. I really didn't have much ambition after that first commitment and was just happy to be done with school. Later I took up the study of the insane, after my first commitment and later in Illinois when your father was stationed there."

I was afraid we were about be subjected to hearing what Markie might have learned about the insane, though she did not identify with the mentally ill. I looked to Teddy for inspired conversation.

"Teddy, what will you have for lunch, how about a hamburger?"

"I want chicken soup and an egg salad sandwich." He was not changing his menu plan today, or any day, from his usual dependable meal. Like his Dad he was loyal to the food he liked and knew. Chicken soup and egg salad could be counted on even if their mother couldn't be here in this place or anywhere.

"And you, Cam?" He was looking down at his napkin and at the empty plate in front of him. He played uneasily with the silverware and my knee under the table with his right foot. With very little restaurant experience to go on he spoke up slowly and in a muffled voice uttered: "Same as Teddy." He would have liked to ask for spaghetti but didn't want there to be any surprises during this luncheon.

"Teddy and Cam, do you remember our apartment in New York? The long skinny hallway and your bedroom just off the hall down front by the front door?" She chuckled a little to herself before starting in again. "All those locks on the doors to make sure no one could enter, especially your father, whom I married twice, and my mother, Muffy, your grandmother, who had six children. Your father is evil, steals money from people and then gives jewels to that awful Jew, your stepmother, Joan Jacoby Roberts."

Cam and Teddy sat stone faced in front of Markie, clearly ignorant of any memory of their time with her. The pain of their exit from their former life via the air raid shelter was obviously so painful that they had erased all memories of domestic life with Markie.

"Markie, do you want to order?" I interrupted in order to abort Markie's harangue.

"Oh, darling, I really don't need to eat much, just coffee. Everything else is so bad for you, dairy products, lettuce and vegetable sprayed in poison and white bread. I try to eat alone or only buy safe products."

Feeling guilty, I ordered a salad with Russian dressing and tried to find a new conversational ground.

"What do you think will happen with the upcoming election?" I posed, wondering if Markie thought much about politics or the national new. Do you think a Catholic can become President?"

Lunch arrived just as Markie was about to give me her answer. I was not prepared for her response.

"That awful family! They were fruit peddlers before they got rich and went into politics. That John should never run this country. And we never should have had that Jew from Hyde Park, New York as President."

In a way I should not have been surprised. My father was not a Kennedy lover either. As wild as my mother could be, her family remained staunchly conservative in its values and its belief in the Republican Party. My Father and Markie were bound to marry a second time when Cam came along for the sake of propriety. Granny Roberts had been a more independent thinker and favored Adlai Stevenson as her political role model.

We hurried through lunch, touching on small talk topics like how tall Teddy

was and how he had no pimples, how cute Cammy was for a seven year old and how I ought to lose a little weight to be most beautiful.

"We really do have to go now. Dad will be waiting for us at Ashmont Station," I lied. I could tell Ted and Cam wanted out of there away from Markie that day, maybe forever.

"Oh, babies, please don't go yet. I must see you again in New York. You must stay with me, come live with me. Tell your father that you must leave his care as long as he stays married to that Jewess."

With hurried farewells and another lying promise to write, we escaped the Red Coach Grille, South Station and our mother. Another sad good bye.

For the next two years I hibernated mentally until my final encounter with the headmistress.

Because of its artsy reputation, the one place I wanted to go to college was Sarah Lawrence in New York and maybe the Peace Corps after graduation.

It came time in the fall of my senior year to decide about college. The process at Milton had not changed in half a century. My advisor, or home room teacher, was a woman named Mrs. Gall, who doubled as my history teacher. Because she was an orphan who had been sent as a young child to live with Milton's athletic coach, I could tell she felt somewhat like a loner, too, and that she liked me and was in my corner most of the time. When I was called to the office of the headmistress for my college interview I knew the head mistress would be less sympathetic.

"Come in. Sit down. How are you?" When I made no answer she got right to the point. "More importantly, how are you with boys?" The headmistress leaned her words into me, putting her hand on my arm which she extended from her desk right next to my chair.

I flashed back to field hockey camp that summer when Jock Peers came to see his little sister, Martha, my bunkmate and Milton classmate with his friend, Fred Flanders. We went to a drive-in and necked all night. Did she somehow have a tape recording of that? I felt I was choking silently.

"Well, I really enjoy playing sports with them, if that's what you mean." I knew that's not what she meant. I stared at her low flying boobs beneath the yellow broadcloth blouse resting comfortably just above her waist inside her manly blue suit.

"Really? That's good to hear. In that case I would like to speak to you on another matter. Your friend Betsy. I want you to stop seeing her because she is a bad influence on you. I take that back. She could be a bad influence on you."

What was she talking about? Betsy was one confused, sweet kid with a much messed up family and a father, who like mine, was too nice and too yielding at times. Neither father ever said no to us, nor exercised often much needed disciplinary action. I was too stunned to argue or object to her assessment.

"Have you thought at all about transferring to another school? I hear the Kent School in Connecticut is opening a new boarding wing. You are either 11th in your class or 22nd in the class out of 37 depending on how you look at this. So many of you are stuck at the B-average level. How do you feel about that?"

What did I think about that? I couldn't think. How did I feel about being taken out of school before finishing at Milton, marked as a mental misfit among the other girls in my class? I thought I was there to talk about college, not about boarding school.

Who had she been talking to? My advisor, Mrs. Getch? Or was it Joan, who wanted to get rid of me? Miss Sullivan, the gym teacher, because I had been smoking in the butt room after hockey practice? I was confused and began to shutdown. I couldn't breathe. My eyes glazed over right there in front of her. I started looking at the wall and hoped to be excused immediately from the office.

"Just a few things for you to think about today. I hope you have a good fall. I will be talking to your parents about all of these things soon."

I was sure I dripped sweat all over the knob as I closed the door. Leave Milton? Why? This is where my friends were. I thought. Were they behind this? Why now with only one year to go? I was not going to go.

I spent a lot of time keeping my devastation to myself. Normally talkative, especially to new students or those I did not know well but wanted to impress, I withdrew. Then there was Polly and Katty and Tib and others, but I no longer went to the butt room.

The one fortunate occurrence that year was that I was chosen to join the members of the Madrigal Society, a group of the twenty best singers in the school. Maybe the music director was being kind, but I had tried be chosen for the group after trying after tryouts. Being affirmed as a good singer probably got me through to my senior year.

By late fall, at home my sullenness reached Joan's breaking point. One night I was sitting alone in the living room when Joan encountered me tickling the piano, picking out the notes for the madrigal "The Silver Swan."

"What are you doing?" She implied that if you are idle you are a lazy bitch. "Nothing." I took my hand off the keys. Joan looked red in the face. Maybe Lucy's retarded antics were getting to her. Lucy had been born premature, had been induced and we figured that the clamps that had been used to pull her out left her with an I.Q of about eighty-five. She could never be left unattended or to fend for herself. Tough for Joan, no doubt.

But the outbursts continued. They came at random moments with no context. Often they started with Joan's first words early in the morning at breakfast before we walked to school. "I am not your housekeeper and I am not leaving. So get used to it!" Then, turning as she spoke, she would bolt from the room, her last sentence trailing like smoke behind her: "Pick up your God damned room!"

One night after I had eaten half of one of Joan's cakes and most of the frosting, I crawled to bed past the phone booth in the hall and my parents' bedroom. On the way, in the bathroom, I found a large bottle of aspirin. I really had no idea why I was doing this except that I was sick and tired of the scenario at home and the pressure at school. I grabbed a handful of white pills, swallowing them down hard with a glass of water. Then another handful and more water, until the bottle was empty.

During the next fifteen hours Joan came to my door once but did not open it. She knocked but did not speak. She probably thought I was sulking, not answering her. My father was out of town. When I woke up the next afternoon, Joan found me vomiting in the bathroom. She opened the door with the empty aspirin bottle raised in her hand like a weapon about to destroy me. "How could you do this to us," she barked, "bring us such shame?" She didn't get it. I was the one who was ashamed, that's why I did it.

"You must tell no one about this, do you hear?" Joan plodded on. "I am not even going to tell your father. He would be so pleased with you." She never asked why I wanted to hurt myself.

No one saw me take the aspirin or ever heard about that day. No ever knew how seriously I wanted to escape. No one except Cassandra. In the last minutes before the aspirin put me into a deep sleep, I sought solace on a page in my journal:

Dear Cassandra:
Nothing is working. I cannot do this anymore. Even the music no longer helps. Good night.

The Glass Is Nearly Full

That was it. I graduated from high school. While most of my classmates went on to college on the east coast, I went west to Saint Louis. I made the Dean's list the first semester much to my surprise. But early spring, 1963, after one semester at Washington University, when an overzealous boyfriend began stalking me, I dropped out, no doubt justifying Milton's headmistress's expectations of me, not only as an underachiever, but as an embarrassment to the Academy. My father couldn't afford college anyway and suggested the Peace Corps as a way to get a worldly education and do the kind of service he loved but could never take time to do.

Moving back to Boston, I lived on Beacon Hill and changed apartments, roommates and jobs for each of the next three years. First I was a nurse's aide, because I naively thought the healing profession would make me "noble."Next I was as an assembly line worker at a Portuguese-owned slipper factory where no one spoke English and the workers giggled behind my back. Then I stacked and sold art books at the Harvard Coop bookstore in Cambridge where I saw lots of attractive Harvard undergraduates though no one seemed interested in asking for a date. In the fall of 1966, after applying twice, I was accepted into the Peace Corps, the only one of 45 women trainees who did not have a college degree. Those six years of French and five years of Latin made me an able linguist. After adding Tunisian Arabic to my skills during training I would soon learn the joys of living in the bilingual country of Tunisia in North Africa.

My father did his best to point me toward good choices. In his own way he could be uncannily and surprisingly smart. In a sense he saved me from going down a dark road, because I could join the Peace Corps and leave my old self behind. In training with girls from all over the country I made a new set of friends, each ready to embrace an entirely new and uncertain experience. Most had come to genuinely help an underdeveloped community survive somewhere on the other side of the world.

I loved every minute of every day of training at Wheelock College in downtown Boston and I couldn't wait to go to Africa. It was as if I had been set free of the judgments of others and of myself. I shined. I became a popular leader. I loved this thing called community development. I had always wanted to make a difference. That's the main thing for me.

At the end of training all but four of us were ready to go. One girl, Rhana Penix, whose last name sounded like "penis" left, because every time her name was called there, was uncontrollable laughter. Although I don't remember her name, another girl decided she was better suited to become a novelist and did. Two other girls left after the first day. But the rest of us were committed to Tunisia Childcare 8.

Our group stood around on the curb outside the Wheelock dorm waiting to get onto the rented yellow bus that would take us to the airport for the flight to New York en route to Tunis. My father was there, of course, and he and I laughed a lot and joked around about nothing in particular. He had taken the morning off to come say goodbye. The winter was mild still, no snow yet even though it was February. The gray herring bone coat hugged his still rugged fifty year- old frame over his pinstriped Brooks Brothers suit, his blue uniform. The collar of the coat was pulled up next to his ears, his only physical oddity. They stuck out like Howdy Doody's and everyone said so. He could make them wiggle like crazy. But to me my father was Paul Newman standing next to me with a big hug.

We boarded the bus and I moved way back so I could see my dad as we drove away. Joan was not there that day. I refused to say goodbye to Joan after my last conversation with her:

"Birth control pills? They are giving you birth control pills? That is a really dumb decision. You will never remember to take them every day."

Thanks but no thanks; I didn't need her good wishes.

When I left for Tunisia I did not know how or where Markie was except for the snippets I gleaned from my encounter with Muffy at the airport in New York. I had not seen her since that lunch in Boston when I had just turned 15. I never saw my uncles, my mother's brothers, Dick and Don, who could tell me about her. I didn't know why, when they lived not far from my family in Milton, we had no contact. I was vaguely uneasy about not being in the know, just as I had been when my brothers were taken away. I didn't know this would be the last time I would see my father, his hands waving at me at the back of the bus like a slow and steady windshield wiper, back and forth, back and forth. *Endlessly reliable and ever loving.* I would relive that goodbye many times over in my dreams before and after his death. It took a long time to let him go.

Caesar's Way

My father's death that Christmas I was in Tunisia in 1967 haunted me for many years, shut away inside me, closed off from any allowable grief, until I moved back to Milton years later. After the Peace Corps, life in Iowa and Japan and the subsequent divorce from John in the early 1970's, I longed for a more predictable and stable life.

In 1974, the same year that John and I divorced, I met my second husband, Tim. Initially, he helped me get a job in public relations for the New York State Association for Retarded Children in New York City where he worked aiding and supporting the families of children with retardation. I had turned down an offer to be a staff writer at *Parade Magazine* because it paid less. This was a big mistake as I soon found that for me interviewing the anguished parents of handicapped children was both too intense and exhausting.

On one of my first days on the job, I was asked to join Tim and several secretaries, for his birthday lunch at a deli near the Flatiron Building that housed our offices. The other ladies in the office adored him for his Southern good manners, his slight drawl and because, having two younger sisters, he seemed to generally understand the female psyche.

Tim resembled Kentucky Fried's Colonel Saunders with laughing grey eyes and a ready smile above his sandy orange beard. In high school, in Columbus, Georgia, he had been considered a very good football player until his teammates grew to tower over his five foot six inch frame. Instead, he became a very good dancer, one of the first things that attracted me to him.

"When am I going to meet the girl of my dreams?" Tim mused over a thick Reuben on rye. I thought this was a silly and fatuous question. The other women just giggled and approved of such a romantic question, probably because none of them had yet been married.

"Are you dating anyone right now?" I asked, but really without interest in knowing the answer.

"No, but I always wanted to marry someone from Boston, someone

150

who could look good in the morning without make up unlike all the made up Southern girls I knew growing up."

Lofty goals for a wife, I thought sarcastically. My first reaction was that he seemed a little shallow for my New England sensibilities that sought more cerebral adventure to keep me interested. Unfortunately, I ignored my initial instinct. In a short period of time we began dating and spending time at parties in the Hamptons with other young professionals looking to escape the city on weekends.

Divorce was still raw and recent for me. I was living alone in a one room flat not far from Tim on the Upper East Side. I was lonely in New York without family to comfort me though I wasn't ready to join forces with Tim when he asked me to move in to his apartment at East 73 and Third Avenue. I moved in anyway, out of insecurity and lack of will to strike out on my own. I was not ready to get serious about any man any time soon. Besides, we had some serious differences.

For one thing, Tim had been a chaplain in Vietnam during the recent war. I had been an avid protester of that war, and all wars, and had been married to a Conscientious Objector long enough to know I was a true "Peacenik." Then, too, our backgrounds were completely different. I was a New Englander with a somewhat entitled Boston attitude, and Tim was a southerner who thought women belonged in a certain role, standing by their men but never in front of them.

There was one other big obstacle in our relationship. I had always been athletic and physically active. Tim observed that I seemed more confident on a tennis court than off and saw this as a weakness that I could play tennis but not deal very well with everyday routine. His criticism eventually drove a silent wedge between us, and I reacted poorly by taking up with a tennis player four years younger than I during the time a number of us shared a weekend house on the beach in the Hamptons.

Embarrassed by my lapse in fidelity, Tim quickly left New York to take a job with the Federal Government in Washington, D.C. A series of trips ensued for me back and forth between Tim in D.C. and the tennis player in New York. At the end of a visit to D.C. over New Year's in 1976, Tim took me to Union Station to say goodbye. We stood together on the platform just before the train rolled out of the station. Tim tilted his head toward mine holding my face gently between his two hands: "You are a terrific woman, but really, you are just too crazy for me" he commented, stepping backward with a smile as he turned to walk away.

That did it. There it was again. C-R-A-Z-Y. Crazy like my mother? No, not crazy like my mother. Inexplicably, I thought I had to prove this to Tim by marrying him.

After I joined Tim in D.C., five months later we were married in May of 1976 at Grace Episcopal Church in Georgetown in a very traditional church wedding. Jimmy Carter had been elected that year and Washington was an exciting place to be. This time I embraced the straight-laced Anglican service and didn't mind that several of Tim's old girlfriends were my bridesmaids. We drove off down Pennsylvania Avenue in a borrowed model T Ford, Tim in his white suit and Panama hat, I in a Twenties style white suit with a matching blue and white turban, a la Zelda Fitzgerald.

On our honeymoon in Saint Croix Tim bought a small baby blanket with a white organdy coverlet and little blue bows, one on each corner of the fabric. Clearly he wanted children right away. When I didn't become pregnant in three months, he suggested a fertility clinic. Luckily I became pregnant early the next spring.

Not really having had a mother, clearly I was not prepared for the maternal road ahead. On my first visit to the doctor I was asked about my mother's pregnancies. How long were her labors? Did she have Caesarian sections or natural child birth? Did she have gestational diabetes? Varicose veins? I had no idea. Curiously, no one asked me about post partum depression. All I asked was could I smoke and continue to coach my little boys soccer team? My questions evoked as few answers as did mine to the doctor's queries.

Luckily, the birth of both of my children helped to strengthen my growing conviction that I might really be healthy and of sound mind.

During my pregnancy Tim and I trained faithfully in the then popular *Lamaze* classes, the prepared childbirth technique developed in the 1940s by a French obstetrician. But, by the time I was three weeks overdue in late December, we knew something was wrong. The doctor was concerned because the baby's head had not yet descended. I was told to prepare for a Caesarian section.

At first I panicked. Isn't that what happened in the end of *A Farewell to Arms* when Catherine Barkley died after three days in labor? Had I

trained in the art of natural childbirth with a wonderful teacher and new friends only to come to this? And didn't my grandmother Muffy birth six children with a homeopath and no real medications? This was not right.

At 9:45 the next morning I waddled down to the nursing station in my faded beige bathrobe and brown knitted slippers. My doctor said "hi" with one eye while he read my chart with the other. Tim joined me to walk the hall with me to the delivery wing.

In the OR a Korean doctor greeted me cheerily. His English left me with the immediate impression I might be thoroughly misunderstood as he guided me through the epidural over the next few hours. However, my fears soon subsided as he began to explain his position on the team of ten who were going to perform the birth miracle ahead. I was confident there were enough translators on hand if need be. He placed an

IV drip in my left arm before proceeding to the epidural.

The doctor was good at telling the attendants what his every move would be. He was a safecracker instructing a protégé as he carefully turned the lock in the key. My adrenalin began to slow down. The IV drip in my left arm was working and I was swimming in and out consciousness.

Barely forty minutes later I heard the doctor's deep basso boom: "It's a girl!" Tears welled up in my eyes as a squirming, beautiful, wet body passed over my head into a warm bath waiting nearby in the corner of the room. I felt joy, but more relief and awe that all was okay. Tim and I had contemplated many choices of names for our first child before that day. Suddenly, out of my mouth popped the words "Pamela, Pamela, Pam."

The nurses rushed to clean Pam up while she cried and kicked furiously. I again counted the people in the room and through my haze marveled that all ten had stayed for the big event. I remarked to the intern how wonderful it was for Pam and me to be totally on stage without any guilt feelings about being the center of attention, a once in a lifetime show! In my delirium, I thanked them all for coming to the party.

When the nurse brought Pam into my room an hour later, I felt almost as innocent and unknowing as the child I held in my arms. Though she couldn't really see me yet, Pam had that quizzical look on her face that I would later recognize as "are we really in this together?" How could it be that she and I had come so far together in such a short time? Becoming a mother, earning to be a mother was a completely new journey for me and I felt at first as if I were drifting into unfathomable waters.

The entries of both of my daughters into this world proved to be two great beginnings. It was also the starting point of a new confirmation of my own life. In the first days and months of Pam's life, I waited constantly for the dark shadow of the albatross to come over me as it did my mother after the birth of each of her children. Several months passed and yet I still did not feel immune. It was only after Dana's birth that I began to feel an inner safety net around me supporting my growing understanding that I was really going to be okay for the long haul.

A Christmas Story

For nearly a decade I held various public relations jobs and wound up working for my old employer, the Peace Corps. Increasingly, Tim and I had visions of moving to New England where he had always wanted to live and I wanted to return. In 1985, I was at a Milton Academy alumni party at the City Tavern in Georgetown when I was approached by the headmaster. He asked if I would like to come to work at Milton in the fundraising office. My children would be able to go to school there tuition free if they were accepted. Miraculously, Tim got an offer in Boston, too, to work for an energy newsletter. At the time, I wondered if my father was looking down from above and making this all possible.

Once back home in Milton, I was reminded of him daily, as if part of him was still here, and began, again, to really grieve for him. I would sit for hours on the porch upstairs outside my bedroom smoking one cigarette after another, glass of wine in hand, looking up into the sky, not looking for anything really, just searching.

It had been years since I lived in Milton as a child. I was no longer the little kid living in the Texas dustbowl, learning to ride a bike and begging for music lessons, nor the little fat girl entering sixth grade at Milton Academy. No longer afraid of the stepmother or a more privileged cousin, I came home a woman. I was fully in the present tense, in charge of my life. The targets were now mine by choice. This was no longer just a training ground where I grew up. This was the real playing field. I was playing the game my mother didn't know how to play and could never show me how. The one regret I still have that will be with me forever is my grief for losing my father without ever saying goodbye to this soft, gentle man.

All the while we were living in Milton, Markie was wandering around the New York City that we had left nearly a decade ago. I had not stayed in touch with her even when my children were born. I did learn later from Muffy that she spent many nights away from her rat infested, government sponsored apartment, preferring to stay with her mother on 79th Street.

155

In 1992, my Uncle Dick, Markie's brother, the artist, informed me that my grandmother, Muffy, had died at age eighty-five. She would no longer be there to pick up the pieces for Markie. The day Muffy died, the real estate broker was ecstatic, because he could now break the 60 year contract on Muffy's rent controlled apartment. Markie somehow wound up in the inpatient care of the Payne Whitney Clinic of New York's Presbyterian Hospital. Subsequently, she suffered a complete disorientation as a result of over medication and neglect by health-care professionals, until my brother Cameron rescued her and brought her to a safe haven in Salem, Massachusetts.

Derby House is named after the street on which it sits facing the harbor. Endowed by some genteel merchants involved in the East India Trade successes, it is an assisted living facility that houses approximately twenty-five ladies who qualify to live there at no expense, having given up all their worldly possessions to the state.

In many ways, Markie was almost normal in the last decade of her life. She became the consummate gentle, wise, witty grandmother. As an exiled patrician, she lived, for all intents and purposes, a reclusive life as the person she wanted to be, a person apart from the world, isolated from the ordinary wear and care that may grind a person down. She seemed perfectly at peace within herself and in her lack of interaction with the world. She still had all those food issues and she hung on to the "begats."

During the early days after Markie arrived at Derby house, in addition to having to fitting in frequent visits to her with my children, I had my own worries at home. After nearly twenty years of marriage, husband Tim was becoming increasingly critical of me as a woman and as a mother. When he insisted I go on a therapeutic weekend to learn how to get along better with men, I knew our marriage was headed for ruin, since the only man I didn't get along with was him.

That year the beginning signs of how each member of our family might react to the break-up of our marriage became evident at Christmas time at our house during the annual trimming of the tree.

Rituals were always important to Tim. They were to me, too, but to a lesser extent because Tim always played the role of the grand master of ceremonies for every birthday, Christmas, Easter or traditional holiday occasion. For Easter, he actually made Greek Easter bread and even put

the colored eggs in the middle of the braided strands of dough. He made birthday cakes for the girls. One in particular was in the shape of a child's bed made with two square layers of yellow cake covered in white frosting made to look like a bedspread with a little doll's head tucked in at the top of the bed cover. The frosted bed cover read "Happy Birthday!" with six candles spaced evenly across the middle of the cake.

Most of all Tim liked to decorate the Christmas tree. He took pride in the many Christmas tree ornaments he had been given by his family, particularly his mother, over the years. There were fragile transparent glass snowflakes that could hang on the end of branches and glisten beneath the tree lights, little bells that jingled before you put them on the tree, dancing elves made from wood carvings and all matter of delicate fanciful ornaments along with the traditional colored glass balls in all shapes and sizes. At the end of the trimming we would throw shreds of silver icicles up around and all over the tree. The result, like his birthday cakes, was truly magical.

That year Matthew, the cat, still lived with us. "Matty" was large and orange, the color of marmalade. Dana adored him. The rest of us had learned to live with him for Dana's sake and had accepted him into the family. Now that he had been with us for two years, there would even be presents under the tree for him.

At around 6:00 pm I arrived home after a forty dollar cab from downtown Boston where I had purchased a small pool table set to surprise the girls on Christmas morning. I snuck in the front door to go upstairs unseen to hide the big box under my bed. Tim and I had not slept in the same room for years so the game table would be a surprise to him, too.

When I came downstairs to the living room, the trimming had already begun. Tim was annoyed that I had not been there for the start of the event. Every year he claimed that I didn't seem interested in trimming the tree. Maybe Tim was right. It even seemed somewhat sacrilegious to be so celebratory on a holiday during which memories of my father still lingered.

Tim placed an angel at the very top of the tree and then began hanging the glass balls just below, moving slowly circling the tree with larger ornaments. One at a time Pam and Dana took turns handing their father the next ornament to be properly placed. This was a real ritual enjoyed by the three of them while I sat on the couch and watched their mutual pleasure. I noticed that Matty had jumped up onto the mantelpiece from the armchair below but seemed peacefully curled up like the Cheshire cat in *Alice and Wonderland.*

No one saw Matty leap at the angel at the top of the tree. Something in the angel's plastic face or the glitter of her wings must have scared him. Instantly the tree fell over. The crash of the delicate ornaments rang out like the opening cadenza of a Beethoven movement. For one moment we were each, separately, but equally frozen and stunned.

Instantly and without thought, I ran down the stairs to the basement to get the vacuum cleaner to clean up the mess and retrieve any undamaged items. Tim began to cry inconsolably. The family history of passed down ornaments was gone forever. When I returned with the vacuum, Pam, the future psychologist was waiting for me. "How could you think about cleaning up at a time like this when we haven't had time to mourn the loss of these things yet?" Embarrassed by my action that she had thought so untimely, I turned away from her in time to catch sight of Dana. She was standing near the front of the room on the other side from where the tree had fallen and was staring out the window, patting her cat and wondering what was coming next. The types of responses of each of us had that night to the crash of the tree and the braking of the ornaments would reappear in similar ways in future family crises.

The following year, as a diversion from the stress of being around Tim, I took up the game of squash. One could get a great workout in a short period of time, and there were good courts at nearby Milton Academy where my children went to school and I worked in the fundraising office. I was introduced to Bob by a venerable schoolmaster who had started the squash program at the school and who hoped that Bob could teach me to play the game. Every weekend for the rest of that year I played squash with him. He always beat me but was generous of spirit and I was appreciative of his encouraging praises of my game. Like me, he had graduated from Milton. He went to Harvard, became a high school teacher and later a headhunter. Two of his three children attended Milton at the same time mine were still there. He was six years older than I and unperturbed by my sometimes noisy outbursts on the court. I had the annoying habit of shouting Helen Reddy's "I am woman hear me roar" on the court whenever I won a point.

Because of the age difference, we had not known each other as teenagers, but we had attended the same dancing school, those same Milton "Sociables" at different times and, later, coming out parties. When I left Boston for Tunisia in the Peace Corps, Bob had just become one of Boston Globe's most eligible bachelors.

In the spring of 1995, Bob's youngest daughter graduated from Milton. Not long after that, Bob's wife of twenty-seven years decided their marriage had lasted long enough. In the first ten minutes of his recounting his dismissal, he told me he was sad. In the next ten minutes he warmed to the thought of the possibility of a new match.

Up until that point in June of 1996, after many squash games I had absolutely no attraction to Bob, only to his racquet skills and occasionally to his thick, very grey-white hair and his less than cool glasses. But that was all. I didn't notice his trim physique or the fact that he was a good deal taller than most men I had known. Very quickly that soon changed, first into a kindred friendship between two souls sharing disappointments in marriage, and then rapidly into a passionate love affair. Following both of our divorces, Bob and I were married in 1997, on the night before Thanksgiving.

Over the next five years, on many Sundays, I drove up from Milton to Salem, past the Salem Witch Museum through the center of town, to pick Markie up at Derby House for Sunday lunch. Some things never change. She would not eat lettuce because it contained lots of the toxins from being sprayed. No meat ever. No sugar. Only spaghetti with butter. She would only eat dinner rolls if the restaurant could assure her that they were made without sugar. She never changed her ways and became more adamant over time. Ignoring her phobias, I maintained my appetite for juicy hamburgers and green salads loaded with the dreaded croutons.

At the end of every visit a special ritual took place when we returned to Derby House Salem wharf. We entered the screen door just inside the porch and faced a daunting line up of ladies sitting in wheel chairs or rockers waiting to greet us in the front room.

"Hello, have you met my daughter Diana? She is the first of my three children whom I had with their father George F. Roberts Senior. Her younger brother George is named for their father whom I married twice you see. Then there is the matter of the youngest brother Cameron Byron

Roberts. My daughter has been married three times, first to John Hodges whom she married in Iowa, of all places, and then to Tim McCartney, who was from Georgia, by whom she had her two children, Pam and Dana. She is now married to Robert Bray, her third husband, who has fabulous hair! " This last comment was her way of affirming, every time we faced those ladies, her positive acceptance of her third son-in-law.

By the third time Markie began this litany on the porch, the ladies began to chime in. Like a Greek chorus they could recite my mother's words on cue and then watch as I burst into laughter at the accuracy with which they could mimic her phrasing and words! Even Markie found the exchange humorous.

All Things Bright and Beautiful

Ralph Von Williams

Now I am back in Milton where I am unable to let my father's memory go, my mother is also here haunting me in all I do even though she is finally gone. I am just beginning to surrender memories of her. Tomorrow I must celebrate the life of one I never called mother, only and always, "Markie."

The night before her memorial service is closing in on me. Instead of sitting down to prepare a eulogy *(is that really what my remarks would be?)* I escape my thoughts and head into Boston in the car after work to a song and dance rehearsal for an upcoming Vincent Show. Feeling very tense, I am not ready for the task ahead of me.

I am on a dance floor in Boston rehearsing for the same kind of show in which Markie performed in 1936. Slowly, almost without movement, I will myself off the couch where I am sitting and waiting to perform onto the dance floor. The show, *Go for the Gold,* is all about the preposterous notion that ladies will tap dance their way to the Olympics.

"Hi, Diana, where ya' been? You're late. We're starting NOW."

I slip into my place in the fourth row just to the left and behind the center marked "x" where the principal characters are lining up to start the finale. The piano patter begins, but instead of moving my feet to the beat I stand still and suddenly blurt out "My mother died today!" It is right at the start of the final number of the show that will bring down the house with all the cast on stage in character and costume in a fabulous tableau.

The lyrics pour from the poised lips of the cast members as they begin to sing in a well-rehearsed amateur way. Right at the point when verse two is to extol the virtues of the Tapping for the Gold, instead of dancing, one by one the members of the cast circle around me, quite out of step with the beat, but slow and in their own rhythm until they close in and form one gigantic hug around me, smothering me softly in a gentle lull of love and relief from the strain of loss.

The singing and the dance steps lift me up. That act of kindness from the Vincent singers and dancers palpably reminds me what the Vincent Club has represented to many women since its founding in 1892: a place of compassionate caring and service to women's healthcare in the community. Maybe this is all too sentimental, but their gesture captured the kind of bonded friendship that exists between philanthropically mined women who get together every year to write and produce creative musicals with bawdy lyrics to promote women's health at Boston's Vincent Memorial Hospital. At the same time the club remains a bastion of Brahmin WASPiness, entitlement and bravado. To me it is a special sisterhood.

The practice dance floor is surrounded by four walls of mirrors allowing the tap dancers to check their steps and the drill team to watch its form. But this day the mirrors are meant for me. I watch everyone watching me bawling my eyes out quietly, while at the same time trying to get into character and the swing of the rehearsal. I feel unable to fully let go and just grieve. We Bostonians are taught to "never let it show and never let it go." Finally I find a method of escape from myself: I faint.

The loss of consciousness is a godsend. It isn't long before I am actually somewhere between awake and a dream. With Markie gone, I feel a new me emerging, no longer the target of an incomplete life or of a wicked stepmother but a full grown version of whom I was meant to be. After all, I got here on my own. Without you, mother. Even when I made bad choices, they became practice sessions for a brighter future. They taught me to take better aim and make better choices the next time. I now choose arrows for my quiver more carefully and keep them close by and hidden.

The piano player and several cast members move me back to the couch where other cast members sit waiting to sing or dance the numbers they have been selected to perform in the show. I am fully awake and know what I am going to say tomorrow.

At eleven o'clock the sunlight streams through the stained glass windows high above the altar of Saint Michael's Church. The Woods Window, as it is called, was given by Mrs. William Lockwood in memory of her parents, Rhodes and Henrietta Woods, who died in 1905. It is in

the form of three panels framing ten saints with a bevy of angels smiling down on those inside each panel.

Actually, there are more stained-glass windows than are there people in the pews below. In the front on the right, where the family enters through a small door from the parish hall, is a colorful window installed by one Ralph Adams Cram in 1916, whose own self portrait appears in the face of Saint Augustine in the main panel. Augustine lived in Africa between 354 and 430 A.D. and was a convert to Christianity. I am told that Mr. Cram, though far less illustrious, was the original architect of the church built in 1899.

Everyone is now seated, waiting for the organist to begin the prelude and the minister to enter from the side door. A memorial service is about to begin for a person who did not believe in organized religion and who would have surely detested Saint Michael and all the angels. Did anyone ever ask her what she believed or what she wanted for an exit? Did anyone ever ask her permission to put her away in any of those mental institutions?

The rector has done a remarkable job of visiting, comforting and understanding a woman he had only met in the last days of her life. He has been able to grasp and fathom a life that never really reached adulthood. He is gentle and kind beyond belief. He is all Ichabod Crane, so tall and skinny, but his utter ease with the Markie's craziness is comforting and reassuring to us all. When it comes to weddings and funerals, he is the consummate performer, because he schools himself, like an actor, in the principal characters involved in every ritual, both secular and sacred. He married me and my Bob with great tenderness and joy. One of the wedding guests commented at the time that "he taught us all about how to love and what committed love is."

The rector enters and the hymn Cameron and I have chosen begins: "All things bright and bee-uuu-ti-ful, all creatures great and small..." Markie loved animals, "God's creatures great and small. Again I am reminded that she preferred horses and dogs to people because you could trust them. She demonstrated this on one of our walks late in her life. We were strolling down the main street in Salem, Massachusetts, when she saw a horse and buggy being whipped by its driver to transport tourists at a faster pace. I was walking slowly with her, my arm linked in hers, when she jerked away from me to scream out at the driver: "Let that horse go, you murderer! You are despicable! Assassin!" In the hymn, she has it her way: all things remain bright and beautiful, every animal no matter how small.

"I am the resurrection and the life, saith the Lord," the rector begins. "He that believeth in me, though he were dead, yet shall he live; and whosoever liveth and believeth in me shall never die." As I said, Markie didn't believe in organized religion. She was too smart for that. Already I begin to wonder if this is the right place to honor her life.

"I know that my Redeemer liveth to himself, and no man dieth to himself. For if we live, we live unto the Lord; and if we die, we die unto the Lord. Whether we live, therefore, or die, we are the Lord's."

How could Markie be the Lord's when she didn't believe in God? Granted, she was spiritual, but she lived and died alone, belonging to no one, not to her family and certainly not to the Almighty. But now in the end Markie is here with her family, her ashes having been placed in a small brass box on an unobtrusive wooden table on the front steps leading up to the altar. White lilies bulge out of a small vase hiding the small wooden container the size of a cigar box that holds all that is left of Markie. Maybe she really isn't here. *She never was here.* The service is for us, those remaining who never really knew her or were with her.

Cameron is first to step to the lectern. I am apprehensive because he has placed a pile of index cards three inches high in front of him right on top of the lectern. Oh my God! *We'll be here for three hours.*

Luckily, Cameron limits his remarks to the chronology of Markie's life: born in Hagerstown, Maryland, the oldest of six children, multi-talented, a debutante in New York and Boston, a professional model and then a jump to her later life living in Salem, Massachusetts.

Cameron is my youngest brother, the one I cared for, protected from Markie's neglect when he was born. He is the one who refers to himself as the "un-son," because he was born after my parents divorced and before they remarried briefly but never lived together. I can still see Cameron as that three year old all over again in blue overalls arriving in Milton after being rescued by my father from the shelter in Brooklyn after one of Markie's meltdowns. I have always seen him as somewhat defenseless and in need of protection. Between siblings there is always a giver and a taker. With Cameron, I am the giver.

Cameron is an architect by training, and artistic by nature. He has a fine eye for details. He has gone down several paths in life that have not all resulted in good choices. In some ways, like our father, he chose a marriage to someone unstable which ended in divorce. The woman would demand alimony for a lifetime, claiming she could not work although she was a well- trained professional. She would become more bizarre over time causing my little brother a lifetime of damage.

In preparing for the memorial service, out of anxiousness, Cameron and I had fought over every detail, each of us trying to put our own imprint on the service: the placement of the urn of cremated ashes, the color of the flowers, and the order of the service. No doubt he is anxious about his own confused feelings. His only concession is to leave the selection of the hymns to me.

Then Dana, the younger of my two daughters, climbs to the lectern to read a poem I have asked her to share. It hasn't been an easy road together, for her and me, but she is doing what she knows I most need her to do now-give of herself for me. Toward the end of the words written by George Santayana I watch Dana's beautiful small hands touch the single page and hear these words from her gentle voice:

"And I scarce know which part may greater be
What I keep of you, or you rob from me."

While she is speaking, I have a flashback of taking Dana and Pam, when they were barely seven and ten, to meet their grandmother in New York, sometime in the spring of 1987. At the time I thought it was important to show my beautiful daughters that their mom was not going to be crazy like her mother, even though their father kept insisting I would be. While my own marriage to Tim was slowly disintegrating in front of my children's eyes, did I have a right to inflict my own fears on my children? This could turn out to be a bad decision.

The visit starts badly. We ride the bus from 57th Street on the Upper East Side straight down to South Ferry. We plan to take the ferry to Ellis and Staten Island and see the Statue of Liberty along the way. Markie is riding beside me with Pam and Dana beside her.

"Diana, have you got some money with you?" Markie begins casually, not pressing too hard. Dana and Pam don't really hear Markie's question and are busy looking out the window onto Madison Avenue at the shops on the Upper East Side. They are excited because they will be seeing the Rockettes the next day. We buy our tickets and board the ferry.

"Mom, why is she asking for your watch and for money, that is not right," Pam whispers in my ear.

Silently I slip my watch off my wrist. I put it in Markie's right hand and curl my fingers over hers while the girls are not looking.

Dana catches my eye at the last second as I close over Markie's knuckles.

"Mom, she scares me. Don't give her money. Don't. That is not right. That is not fair. She did not take care of you when you were our age," Pam admonishes precociously. I am stunned by my daughter's sense of right and wrong. But the deed is done. I know I will be giving Markie more money and more of me before this trip is over.

We ride the bus in an uncomfortable silence for what seems a long time. Suddenly, as we are passing Lady Liberty in a voice that could have come from the megaphone of a head cheerleader Markie lets rip "ROO-SEV-ELT WAS a JEW!! ROOO-SEV-El-T WAS A JEWWWWWWW!"

On some visceral level, my mother hated Franklin Roosevelt. Actually, many WASPs hated him for "betraying" their social status and class. My father and Markie were united on this point if no other. Whether because of Roosevelt's upbringing or his actions as President, Markie felt an uncontrollable manic urge to let the world know her opinion of him.

Now sitting in the church I soak in this day as I watch Pam move to the lectern, with all the poise of a fully formed adult. It seems just an instant in time since her dramatic entrance into this world. She faces the congregation, if you can even call it that, more like a sparse private audience. She is focused and prepared for her remarks. I wonder how wise or unwise it was of me to bring my children face to face with Markie in that first meeting. Was it fair to rob them of the innocence of youth just so that I could show them that unlike my crazy mother, I was sane and strong and capable? Were they, like me, forced to grow up too soon, to be women before being children?

I notice Pam already has that same get-down-to-business look her mother learned to acquire. And she is only twenty-two. She has chosen to read from a letter she received from her grandmother when she was eight

years old. She has chosen to read a letter she received from her grandmother when she was eight years old.

As I sit there I have an acute memory about my vulnerability and questionable capacity for motherhood without the benefit of motherly advice. A very special interaction with Pam came back to me to call my efforts into question.

Five o'clock. I pick Pam up outside her classroom on the lower school campus. We ride to Osco's talking about the day. I uh-huh in all the right places as I listen to the sound of an ailing carburetor against a background of NPR news. How long has it been since I bought toilet paper for the house or socks or sneakers for the girls? The feeling of how compressed our time is together, what with classes and other concerns, always bugs me. Because of this we do things sometimes more directly with each other, sometimes more openly, often without transition. As we glide through the glass doors of Osco's, we grab a waiting cart and head for the bins of pink and purple socks in the last aisle in the back of the store. Past the detergents, the dog food and the deodorants our cart rests for a moment in the toy section. Cheerfully my daughter she knows that after socks I am a pushover for something special for her. At this hour at the end of the day, I am tired and weak willed.

Sometimes children have a way of being bright and clear and brief at the most astonishing times. When parents are thinking mundane, daughters are thinking monumental. Today, closing in on the last aisle at Osco's, is one of those times. Slowly, unmistakably, there begins a Socratic inquiry from the mind of my nine-year old. As I reach for a pair of purple socks, it starts without introduction:

"Mom, is there a Santa Claus? I really don't think so because I saw you taking out the box that came with Dana's table and chair set last week."

The socks are the wrong color, though we both like the style. I hold them up for us both to look at while I stall for time to frame my Socratic response.

"Pam, do you always answer your own questions?" Not really a good start, but worth about thirty seconds.

"Well, no, but is there?"

Do all nine-year olds begin the search for truth this way? On uncertain ground I rummage through more pairs of socks and looking at different sizes and shapes. One pair catches my attention, emblazoned with sparkles and covered in jagged pink letters broadcasting the current elementary schoolgirl idol, Shera. Looking at Shera gives me the courage to start again. Surely, I can do better than she would.

"Well," I begin, "when we are little, everything is real. Santa Claus is a real person in a loud red suit that brings presents every year on time." As I speak, I am reminded of the crowds I faced a few days before in this very same place for the sake of that red suit. I am wondering if this is a sufficient beginning. As in my classroom, I feel strangely, even here in this department store, that sense of responsibility as a teacher to speak with a moral voice, to provide the proper pearl of wisdom, articulate clearly the right answer.

"As we grow older we take that person and draw him inside us. He becomes a spirit. We learn to give as well as to receive."

Silence. We push our cart along together, each of us dragging one foot on the rung below so our steps can have the same pace. I wait to see how my answer has been received, replaying in my head the sound of my own words, not sure I have solved the problem.

"I like that answer," says Pam in a matter-of-fact tone and with conviction. My daughter has no idea how grateful I am for this affirmation of my small wisdom. We are nearing the end of the aisle. "I really don't respect a mother who won't tell her child the truth," she adds. I am almost ecstatic from approval and think we have ended our discussion.

One can never be too careful at these moments. These occasions are laden with importance masquerading as chit chat. The kids at school are cautious, less inquiring than I would have them be. The classroom is predictable, safe, but in this dance there is no warning, and I am unprepared for the next steps. Suddenly, with no lapse in logic from my daughter, comes the next question.

"Does that mean there's no pink bunny that comes at Eastertime to bring us eggs he didn't lay?"

What's this, the Inquisition? I wheel our cart, slowly, measuring my steps, back to the middle of the store. I wonder how long this child has

been carrying these inquiries around with her, saving them for the right moment of our moments together. And this is not the last question.

"Maybe that's enough for one day, Mom. I don't think we're ready to talk about the birds and the bees."

How right she is. "What about the birds and the bees?"

"You know, S-E-X." Can the same kid who loves Shera be asking this? "What about S-E-X?"

"Well, Mom, if you don't know, you're not ready to talk about it!"

Past the cashier I barely notice the items adding up. I am thinking of my daughter and her skillful, thoughtful ways. The connections she so easily makes between what she needs and wants to know. Her timing is wonderful. I glimpse today's headlines as we pass the newsstand in front of the checkout counter: CHERNOBYL DISASTER LEAVES 4,000 DEAD, 350,000 RESETTLE ELSEWHERE.

I imagine the overwhelming suffering in this nuclear accident and the future world these displaced innocents must face. The numbers swirl in my mind with my child's questions about the future of her own world. The cash box clicks open, the small change comes back to me and a slow rhythm begins in my head. The solution is suddenly here. My child has shown me way. Don't be a cynic. Like a child, always play it straight! I am ready for tomorrow.

Pam faces the small congregation, focused and prepared for her remarks. She begins; clear eyed and slowly, no fear in this moment of speaking before others. She is reading a letter from Markie.

July 23, 1985

Well, Pam:

I want to tell you I got the surprise of my life
when I received your precious letter. How did you do it?
I can't understand—because I never wrote a letter until
years after I was in first grade.
Maybe that was because my first grade was in

an English school in France. The place was Cannes in
France where my parents were spending the winter.
I like that a lot—the place, Cannes. It's in the southern
part of France. And my father rented a lovely villa

There (the Villa Madie).
Villa is what houses are called in France.
I liked the Fontaine School, too. I must have because
I can't remember anything I <u>didn't</u> like about it.
Well my precious little granddaughter—the very first—
The one whose birthday made me a grandmother—of two
precious little girls of my daughter Diana. I love you
all so much!
I hope you will like living around Boston. My
Mother and Father spent some winters there when
I was a child and I liked it very much.
Please give my love to your little sister Dana.
You are so lucky to have her. And to my daughter Diana,
your mother who is the oldest of my three children.
I'm sure at your age you probably know and
Remember your uncles- my two sons--
George French Roberts, Jr. and Cameron
Byron Roberts. The name Cameron is <u>my</u>
father's (Edward J. Byron, Sr.) mother's maiden name.
Well, I want to send all my love to you my
precious first little grandchild, Pam.
From your grandmother.

Markie

P.S. My parents lived in Europe at two different times—
several years apart. What I have mentioned to you
in this letter is only part of the time we were in Europe
the first time.

"Well, done," I whisper to Pam as she returns to her place beside me in the pew. "Very sweet."

That delightful letter was written in 1985, two years before our disastrous ride with Markie on the Staten Island ferry in New York. It was a well written and appropriate letter to an eight-year old. It would be ten years before Cameron would find Markie at the Payne Whitney Clinic in New York. He said that when he first saw her she appeared to be way over-medicated, disoriented and disheveled. Her face, covered in talcum powder, was smeared, not blotted. Her hands were raw from rubbing them together and she moved her tongue aimlessly from side to side. She smelled of urine and staff neglect. Cameron sought and got permission to release her and bring her to Brook House in Salem, Massachusetts. Within months, she was off all medications and on the road to, if not full sanity, at least increased clarity and calm.

My turn at the lectern is coming. Pam is still speaking, but have I stopped listening. I wonder if I have labored long or hard enough to know what to say. For countless hours since Markie's departure, I have been searching for the right words whose meaning would be true to her and still true to me.

I tried to put things in perspective. It has been a seventeen years since I returned to Milton. I have been in this church week after week for years, and yet here, for this purpose today, I feel I am for the first time a part of this quaint little church built in a bygone era, graced by Pierces, Robertses and Byrons before and future generations to come.

In an attempt to steady my nerves I try my gimmick of becoming a part of my surroundings. I recall all the details about this place I have gathered over time. I remember from past funerals you can tell a lot about a funeral by the cars parked outside. For one thing, if there are a lot of cars, the deceased probably had many friends or was very important. If there are a Volvos, BMWs and Audis the person probably traveled in wealthy circles. If there are lots of young people the deceased probably had lots of children and hence grandchildren attend the funeral. There's always one ancient Ford station wagon with ersatz wooden panels, owned by the richest, cheapest widow in town, who would never think of spending her money on a fancy car and actually likes her gas guzzler. She also prefers to keep the holes in her sweaters and attend church wearing her glasses on a chain around her neck that resembles so a set of Greek worry beads. She has come today because funerals for her are like going to the movies. They are her form of entertainment, like going to the movies, even if she doesn't know the main character.

From the outset, there is very little you can tell about the main character at this funeral. There are a few cars, a few flowers and very few visitors. At best maybe three pews on either side of the church are sparsely filled with a handful of family members and one old couple who knew the deceased and her husband when they all lived in New York in the mid 1940's. I am thankful Pam's words were those of my mother and that Cameron did not read the index cards. As Pam steps down, I move slowly to take my place at the lectern.

I put down the paper on which I had prepared my remarks and then hear myself begin:

"My earliest memories of my mother Markie center on her as a very good mother of young children, partly because she was so very childlike herself. In her presence, there was always a wink and a smile for you." This start is the most positive I can make.

"After age nine, when Markie was just 36, I saw her only once again before my own children were born. But as you heard Pam say, she did write. Lots and lots of letters. Some never sent. She loved that I was in the Peace Corps representing the best of America, even as she worried that I would marry a Tunisian or an African. She wrote a very special letter at the time of my father's death, acknowledging how hard it must be for me to be so far away during his illness. When I worked in Japan, she didn't understand how I could work with the Japanese on a Japanese paper because of Pearl Harbor and World War II."

"When I was thirty-two, before Pam was born, the doctors asked me about my medical history. I realized then that I had no idea about my mother's own genes, which could have been passed on to me."

"I was thirty-six when Dana came along and I really wanted to connect with Markie about raising my own children. I was lucky enough to be able to introduce both daughters to their grandmother and their great grandmother Muffy. A snapshot shows the four generations of us sitting in a row on my grandmother's faded salmon silk sofa from so long ago. We had high tea with high cholesterol everything from brie to crème fraiche

and sticky sweet Manachewitz wine that Muffy insisted on. They were both bright and cerebral women whose lives had been marked by faint memories of privileges of a life that had passed them by. The material life was gone. But the attitude remained intact. Muffy was the Queen bee and Markie was ever the Princess in waiting. She spent her life in recluse. Waiting. Until the end.

"Markie may not really have come into her own until Muffy died at eighty-five and Markie moved to Brooke House in nearby Salem, Massachusetts. By her own admission, Markie was always shy and preferred people one on one and animals to people in general. But when she talked with you, it was as if no one else existed in the world at that moment. She was always your best supporter, punctuating her sentences with "fabulous" whenever you mentioned one of your minor successes. She came to enjoy the role of family matriarch, such as it was, as well as the love of the ladies of the Brooke House who adored her. In the last years of her life, when I visited her at Brooke House, I grew to appreciate what wonderful qualities she leaves with us now.

"Markie was always all about *style*. She was a model in New York in her twenties. She became a grand dame of sorts in her own way. To me, she was much more modern than matronly. She was what I call, "a stylin' babe." She had a healthy vanity which in retrospect I now find just great! She wore her threads in the manner of a gracefully aging Greta Garbo who also lived in New York. Sleek velvet pants hugged her slender frame even in her eighties below a tweed or leather jacket. And then there was always some kind of cap to cover the hair she claimed never went gray and was never dyed. Even at the end she was after me to find her a great "brass-iere" that she could wear to fill out what had been her left breast now just an empty cavern left by surgery. And every time I came to Brooke House, she would ask me to get her a new lip liner, forgetting that I had brought one the time before. It was our little game around her need to feel good even in her diminished circumstances. She played it to the hilt every time.

"Markie leaves behind a sense of her great character. To begin with she was the original student of genealogy. She could have written the Book of Genesis- if only she believed in God or the Old Testament.

"She had a dramatic way of saying "so nice to see you, Baby!" She always called us "babies." She even called my husband, Bob, the babe with the "fabulous head of white hair."

"And Markie had a great sense of humor, even at the last. When I would talk about my passion for just about all forms of sport, she would challenge me with the fact that she didn't believe in exercise, period. Only the genes mattered. "I never walk anywhere and always take a cab." She would mention she thought I had "good lines and great bones." She would talk about how much she loved George Bush I but not George Bush II. She didn't like the wife of either and said they had no sense of style. In one visit, she told me again how special each of us children was to her. She called us the best products of her two marriages to the same man."

"On the last day I spent with her I sat by her bedside waiting for the hospice care worker to arrive for her first visit. I sat for a long time in the plastic coated chair opposite her bed and watched her sleeping comfortably.

"Suddenly, Markie's eyes opened wide, as if not on their own accord, and seemed clearer than they had been for many days. In the peace and quiet of the afternoon without knowing where it came from I whispered softly: "Have you been happy?"

"In a very slow, calm voice, clearly her own with that old New York aristocratic tone, I heard Markie pour forth: "Oh, noooooooooh, Diana, the goal is not happiness. The goal of a lifetime is to survive." Then, as she drifted off to mortal sleep, she said she was going off soon to see George, the father of her three children. Some bonds never break. An hour later I thanked and dismissed the lady from hospice care because there was no need anymore.

"Markie's most rational moment may have been her last. Markie lived her life utterly without self-pity or regret. That was her greatest legacy, a gift to me, and all of us. Which I hope you find, as I do, remarkable.

"This has been a very long good bye, not just today on this, her final day, but every day since the beginning. From the start I did not know her well. I did not know her long. I do not judge her now for those years that I lived with her and the years I could not. At the end, now in death, I am glad that she is at peace. And that I, too, am free. *The Albatross has finally fallen and drifted away.*

"The self-same moment I could pray:
And from my neck so free
The Albatross fell off, and sank
Like lead into the sea."

CPSIA information can be obtained
at www.ICGtesting.com
Printed in the USA
LVHW051658290422
717544LV00007B/206